KU-083-769

Pocket
OSLO

P SIGHTS • LOCAL LIFE • MADE EASY

4 3 0006398 8

In This Book

QuickStart Guide

Your keys to understanding the city – we help you decide what to do and how to do it

Need to Know
Tips for a smooth trip

Neighbourhoods
What's where

Explore Oslo

The best things to see and do, neighbourhood by neighbourhood

Top Sights
Make the most of your visit

Local Life
The insider's city

The Best of Olso

The city's highlights in handy lists to help you plan

Best Walks
See the city on foot

Oslo's Best...
The best experiences

Survival Guide

Tips and tricks for a seamless, hassle-free city experience

Getting Around
Travel like a local

Essential Information
Including where to stay

Our selection of the city's best places to eat, drink and experience:

◉ **Sights**

✖ **Eating**

● **Drinking**

✪ **Entertainment**

🔒 **Shopping**

These symbols give you the vital information for each listing:

⏲ Telephone Numbers	👪 Family-Friendly
⏱ Opening Hours	🐾 Pet-Friendly
P Parking	🚌 Bus
⊖ Nonsmoking	🚢 Ferry
@ Internet Access	M Metro
🌐 Wi-Fi Access	🚊 Tram
🥗 Vegetarian Selection	🚆 Train
📋 English-Language Menu	

Find each listing quickly on maps for each neighbourhood:

Bar Hemingway

16 ● Map p233, B2

Legend has it that Hemi
self, wielding a machine
rate this timber-pan
ered bar during
showpiece is a
en by Papa ar
town. Dress
s.com; Hôtel Rit
⏱6.30pm-2a

6 ◉ Plac
V

Lonely Planet's Oslo

Lonely Planet Pocket Guides are designed to get you straight to the heart of the city.

Inside you'll find all the must-see sights, plus tips to make your visit to each one really memorable. We've split the city into easy-to-navigate neighbourhoods and provided clear maps so you'll find your way around with ease. Our expert authors have searched out the best of the city: walks, food, nightlife and shopping, to name a few. Because you want to explore, our 'Local Life' pages will take you to some of the most exciting areas to experience the real Oslo.

And of course you'll find all the practical tips you need for a smooth trip: itineraries for short visits, how to get around, and how much to tip the guy who serves you a drink at the end of a long day's exploration.

It's your guarantee of a really great experience.

Our Promise

You can trust our travel information because Lonely Planet authors visit the places we write about, each and every edition. We never accept freebies for positive coverage, so you can rely on us to tell it like it is.

QuickStart Guide 7

Explore Oslo 21

Worth a Trip:

The Best of Oslo 125

Oslo's Best Walks

Oslo's Best ...

Survival Guide 143

QuickStart Guide

Welcome to Oslo

Surrounded by mountains and the sea, this compact, cultured, caring and fun city is Europe's fastest-growing capital. Come and experience this newly confident boom town as its reputation as a Neo Nordic culinary star, contemporary art centre and live music hotspot grows and grows.

Barcode district, Bjørvika (p126)
DIGITALMAMMOTH/SHUTTERSTOCK ©

Oslo
Top Sights

Oslo Opera House (p48)

Inspiring contemporary Norwegian architecture.

CESCASSAWIN/GETTY IMAGES ©

JTB PHOTO/UIG VIA GETTY IMAGES ©

Nasjonalgalleriet (p24)

Munch's *The Scream* and much more.

Royal Palace (p28)

Pretty, friendly palace in beautiful parkland.

Akershus Festning (p26)

Oslofjord views and military history.

Astrup Fearnley Museet (p52)

Big-name international art and architecture.

Vikingskipshuset (p54)

Three Viking ships and a long history.

Vigelandsanlegget (p66)

Thousands of sculptures and the circle of life. *Monolith* by Gustav Vigeland

Holmenkollen Ski Jump (p80)

This edgy architectural mascot overlooks the city, promising snowy good times to all below.

◯ Oslo Local Life

*Local experiences and hidden gems
to help you uncover the real city*

This is a relaxed, cultured city with fabulous nightlife, a booming creative scene, brilliant food and nature on its doorstep. Locals know how to enjoy themselves and take pride in their easy access to both the outdoors and culture.

Bar-Hopping in the City Centre (p30)

☑ Everything in easy strolling distance
☑ All bars are open until super late

Strolling Frognerparken (p70)

☑ Surreal sculpture
☑ Genteel westside lifestyle

Alternative Grünerløkka (p84)

☑ Edgy galleries ☑ City's best bars and cafes

Eastside Wandering (p104)

☑ Historic streets ☑ Multicultural life

Other great places to experience the city like a local:

Winter Wonderland (p34)

Summer Rooftops (p42)

Secret Strøget (p44)

The Fashion Quad (p46)

Waterfront Shopping (p58)

Westside Eating (p77)

Norwegian Wood Festival (p78)

Fairytale Crossing (p89)

Parklife (p93)

Multicultural Shopping (p110)

Oslo
Day Planner

Day One

Start your day with Edvard Munch's *The Scream* at the **Nasjonalgalleriet** (p24) then stroll down Nedre Slottsgate, through the 17th-century grid of Kvadraturen to **Akershus Festning** (p26), where you can wander for free and take in the view.

Head to waterfront **Pipervika** (p60) for a lunchtime feast of Norwegian seafood. Then take the ferry to the pretty Bygdøy Peninsula, spending your afternoon with the three 9th-century vessels on show at the **Vikingskipshuset** (p54).

Book or arrive early for a table at **Sentralen Restaurant** (p37) to enjoy some of the city's most accessible Neo Nordic small plates and excellent wines. Finish your evening off bar-hopping in Yongstorget and around, with cocktails at **Himkok** (p43) (note: it's an unmarked door), then kicking on at indie-paradise **Mono** (p31) or laneway bar **Angst** (p31).

Day Two

Poke around the deliciously ostentatious home of playwright Henrik Ibsen at the **Ibsen Museet** (p34), then wander the **Slottsparken** (p34) and take a **Royal Palace** (p28) tour. Visit the **Queen Sonja Art Stable** (p34) for contemporary art and an insight into Norwegian royal life.

Indulge in that old Norwegian favourite of pizza at the beautiful parkside functionalist building **Kunstnernes Hus** (p119), before heading back through the city to the waterfront and strolling along Akker Brygge to the island of Tjuvholmen. Here you can check out the superstar contemporary-art collection of **Astrup Fearnley Museet** (p52) as well as the surrounding **Tjuvholmen Sculpture Park** (p57).

Then head to **Vingen** (p60) for casual dining with a view, as well as some of the city's best cocktails, before strolling back through the city to **Fuglen** (p119) for more cocktails and great tunes, then a civilised last drink on the terrace at **Tekehtopa** (p118).

Short on time?
We've arranged Oslo's must-sees into these day-by-day itineraries to make sure you see the very best of the city in the time you have available.

Day Three

☀ Climb the roof of the spectacular **Oslo Opera House** (p48) for views and its beautiful architectural details. Then head inside for a **tour** (p49). A quick tram ride from Central Station will take you to Grünerlokka.

☀ Head to **Mathallen Oslo** (p89) for a mix-and-match lunch then stroll around Vulkan. Cross the Alkerselva back into Grünerlokka for an excellent **Tim Wendelboe** (p94) coffee. Take in the shops then head to the **Munchmuseet** (p108), where you can further explore the Oslo of the late 19th century through Munch's eyes.

☾ Experience Neo Nordic dining at its coolest and hang with the local foodie mafia at **Brutus** (p109), a Tøyen trendsetter, then bar-hop from **Pigalle** (p110) to **Dattera Til Hagen** (p111) in Grønland. Then it's back to Grünerlokka for a live act at **Parkteatret** (p98) or dancing at **Blå** (p98).

Day Four

☀ Wander among the bold, sensuous statues of Gustav Vigeland in **Vigelandsanlegget** (p70) in sprawling **Frognerparken** (p70) – go early to enjoy it at its prettiest and least crowded.

☀ Tram over to St Hanshaugen to proud and produce driven **Smalhans** (p118). Play 'I spy' and spot **Holmenkollen Ski Jump** (p81) watching over the city (or jump on the T-bane and head up there for incredible views and a skiing museum).

☾ Go totally traditional for dinner at Grønland's **Olympen** (p110) beer hall. Scoot across the train tracks and grab a 100kr standing-room ticket for a ballet or opera performance and experience the **Oslo Opera House** (p48) in all its glory. Then wander back into the city centre for some serious nightlife.

Need to Know

**For more information,
see Survival Guide (p143)**

Currency
Norwegian kroner (kr)

Language
Norwegian

Visas
Generally not required for tourist stays of
up to 90 days, nor for members of EU or
Schengen member countries.

Money
Banks with ATMs are found throughout the
city centre. Most shops, restaurants, bars
and cafes prefer debit or credit cards over
cash, even for small purchases.

Mobile Phones
Local SIM cards are widely available,
including at the airport, Central Station,
7-Eleven stores and some Narvesen kiosks.
There are three mobile-service providers:
Telenor Mobil, Telia and Chess A.

Time
Central European Time (GMT/UTC plus two
hours)

Tipping
Tipping on a North American scale is not
expected and can be considered embarrassing
to do so. That said, if the service has been
particularly helpful in a midrange to top-end
restaurant, 5% is generally appropriate, and
10% is considered generous.

① Before You Go

Your Daily Budget

Budget: less than 1500kr
▶ Budget hotel room: from 800kr
▶ Hot dog: 30kr
▶ Single tram, bus and train ticket: 33kr
▶ Small beer: 45kr

Midrange: 1500–3000kr
▶ Midrange hotel room: 1200kr
▶ Caffè latte: 45kr
▶ Museum entrance: 100kr
▶ Casual dinner small plate: 130kr
▶ Glass of wine: 95kr
▶ Return ferry to Bygdøy museums: 65kr

Top End: more than 3000kr
▶ Top-end hotel room: from 2500kr
▶ Degustation Neo Nordic dinner: 525–750kr
▶ Three-day Oslo Pass: 745kr
▶ Music festival day ticket: 950kr
▶ Oslofjord cruise: 650kr

Useful Websites

Lonely Planet (www.lonelyplanet.com/oslo)
Destination information and hotel bookings.

Visit Oslo (www.visitoslo.com) Official tourist-
board website; comprehensive and reliable.

Osloby (restaurantguiden.osloby.no) The
city's food scene in detail.

Advance Planning

Three months before Book for fine-dining
Maaemo or Kontrast; buy tickets for summer music festivals.

One month before Check the city's live-
music-venue listings; book hotels.

One week before Book neighbourhood
restaurants; check weather for packing.

2 Arriving in Oslo

Oslo Gardermoen International Airport
Oslo's main airport is 50km north of the city.
The airport is serviced by the high-speed
train service Flytoget (www.flytoget.no;
adult/child 180/90kr) as well as standard
NSB intercity and local trains. The bus
service **Flybussen** (www.flybussen.no) also
runs directly to the centre, with stops around
the city.

DFDS Seaways Port All ferries arriving from
Denmark disembark here. Bus 60 stops
within a couple of minutes' walk of the terminal or it's a short taxi ride from most hotels.

Oslo Sentral All trains from Sweden arrive
and depart from here and it's serviced by
T-bane, trams, buses and taxis.

3 Getting Around

All public transport is covered by the Ruter
(https://ruter.no/en) ticketing system.

🚋 Tram
Oslo's tram network is extensive and runs
24 hours.

🚈 T-bane
All T-bane lines pass through the Nationalthe-
atret, Stortinget and Jernbanetorget (for Oslo
S) stations.

🚌 Bus
There's no central, local bus station, but most
buses converge at Jernbanetorget in front
of Oslo S. Most westbound buses, including
those to Bygdøy and Vigeland Park, also stop
immediately south of the National Theatre.

Service frequency drops dramatically at
night, but on weekends the night buses N12,
N14 and N18 follow the tram routes until 4am
or later; there are also weekend night buses
(201 to 218).

Oslo Pass (p147) holders can travel for free
on all daytime routes in the city centre.

🚲 Bicycle
Oslo City Bike (https://oslobysykkel.no) gives
you unlimited rides of 45 minute duration
over 24 hours, three days or the season
(45/99/299kr). Buy passes online or on
smartphones. Bikes are only available from
6am to midnight and only in the 'ice-free'
season, generally from April to December.

🚤 Boat
Ferries to the Oslofjord islands sail from
Vippetangen Quay. Ferry 91 to Bygdøy leaves
from Rådhusbrygge Quay from March to
October (Map p33).

Boat 62 connects Oslo with Drøbak and other
Oslofjord stops en route, including Håøya for
swimming and camping. It departs from Aker
Brygge Pier (Map p33).

Oslo Neighbourhoods

Frogner & Western Oslo (p64)
Stately, serene Frogner and the surrounding neighbourhoods are home to Gustav Vigeland's famed sculpture park.

◉ Top Sights
Vigelandsanlegget

Central Oslo (p22)
Oslo's centre is easily walkable and packed with some of the city's most stellar cultural offerings.

◉ Top Sights
Nasjonalgalleriet
Akershus Festning
Royal Palace

Aker Brygge & Bygdøy (p50)
Museums make Aker Brygge and Bydøy peninsula destinations in themselves, as do the waterfront bars and restaurants.

◉ Top Sights
Astrup Fearnley Museet
Vikingskipshuset

◉ **Vigelandsanlegget**

Astrup Fearnley Museet ◉

◉ **Vikingskipshuset**

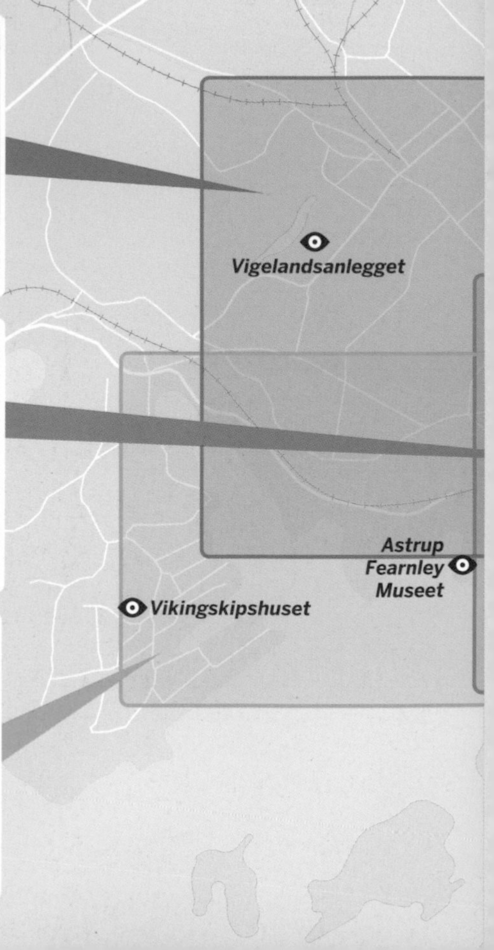

St Olafs Plass, Bislett & St Hanshaugen (p112)
Residential by nature, these neighbourhoods are known for locally-ordained eating and drinking strips, including some legendary cafes.

Worth a Trip
⊙ Top Sights
Oslo Opera House
Holmenkollen Ski Jump
Day-tripping to Fredrikstad

Grünerløkka & Vulkan (p82)
These neighbourhoods are the city's young heart, with the best bars, restaurants, venues and indie shops.

Royal Palace
⊙

⊙ *Nasjonalgalleriet*

⊙ *Akerhus Festning*

⊙ *Oslo Opera House*

Sofienberg, Grønland & Tøyen (p102)
These neighbourhoods are up and coming, emerging and gritty, but vibrant and fun places to visit.

Explore
Oslo

Worth a Trip

Rådhus (p36), Aker Brygge
MAREMAGNUM/GETTY IMAGES ©

Explore

Central Oslo

Oslo's centre is compact, character-filled and easily walkable. Its main street, Karl Johans gate, runs a ceremonial axis east–west from Central Station to the Royal Palace. While it's always been lively and well loved by locals as well as visitors, it's now even more so, with clusters of new places to shop, eat and drink springing up.

JEAN-PIERRE LESCOURRET/GETTY IMAGES ©

The Sights in a Day

☀️ Start your day by getting face-to-face with one of the world's most notorious paintings, Edvard Munch's *The Scream,* along with a number of his other most famous works at the **Nasjonalgalleriet** (p24). Head to the Grand Hotel's **Grand Café** (p37) for an early lunch.

☀️ Time now to visit the beloved Norwegian royals at their buttercup-coloured neoclassical **Royal Palace** (p28), and, if it's summer, take a tour of its evocative interiors and the charming **Queen Sonja Art Stable** (p34). Stroll the Royal Palace's lush and woody parkland **Slottsparken** (p34) and laze on the grass by its pretty lake before catching a tour of Ibsen's luxe apartment at the **Ibsen Museet** (p34).

🌙 Then head to **Akershus Festning** (p26) for Oslofjord views, the beautiful Renaissance-era castle and other exhibits at Oslo's sprawling medieval fortress. Check out **Sentralen** (p30)'s contemporary architecture, swing past the **Parliament Building** (p37) and the **Rådhus** (p36) before dinner at waterfront **Solsiden** (p40).

For a local's day in Central Oslo, see p30.

👁 Top Sights

Nasjonalgalleriet (p24)

Akershus Festning (p26)

Royal Palace (p28)

🔍 Local Life

Bar-Hopping in the City Centre (p30)

❤️ Best of Oslo

Eating

Sentralen Restaurant (p37)

Sentralen Cafeteria (p39)

Grand Café (p37)

Theatercafeen (p41)

Illegal Burgers (p40)

Drinking

Himkok (p43)

Røør (p44)

Kulturhuset (p42)

Oslo Camping (p44)

Getting There

🚇 **Train** Oslo's underground train system fans out from Central Station.

🚊 **Tram** Most of the city's tram lines converge outside Central Station.

Top Sights
Nasjonalgalleriet

The nation's most extensive collection of art, from antiquities to modernism, is housed in the neoclassical pile of the Nasjonalgalleriet (National Gallery). It's an impressive collection indeed, but while you'll find the lovely Lucas Cranachs, fair-to-middling Picassos and Claudel's comely *Head of a Girl* sculpture delightful, it's *The Scream* everyone is here to see.

Map p32, C3

21 98 20 00

www.nasjonalmuseet.no

Universitetsgata 13

adult/child 100kr/free

10am-6pm Tue, Wed & Fri, to 7pm Thu, 11am-5pm Sat & Sun

Tullinløkka

The Scream

Let's not pretend you'll get the world's second most famous painting all to yourself. That said, unlike No 1, the Louvre's *Mona Lisa*, it's not overly armoured (there's just one sheet of protective glass), there's no 20-deep iPhone-waving scrum and there's hardly a queue at the ticket booth. Edvard Munch's 1893 hypnotic, pulsating depiction of existential dread might have become a visual cliché, but it's an incredibly powerful work to confront in real life.

Wall-to-Wall Munch

The Munch room is densely hung in an almost traditional salon style, the works lining up against a deep blue background. While most visitors gravitate to *The Scream*, flanking it are a number of far-from-inconsequential works, and in many respects, better paintings. The transitional semi-naturalist *Puberty* is as shocking and queasy-making today as it must have been in 1895, as is its companion piece, the sensual, manifestly erotic *Madonna*. *Melancholy* combines Munch's extraordinary ability to render psychological states via landscape and his almost cinematic use of suggested narrative. In the face of all Munch's later glorious, hammy semi-abstraction, it's easy to overlook his extraordinary ability as a natural-ist, which can be seen in *The Sick Child*.

Planning for the Future

The Nasjonalgalleriet, the contemporary art Mu-seet for Samtidskunstfour, the Museum of Design and Decorative Arts and the Museum of Archi-tecture were merged in 2003, the first step of a transition to an all-arts Nasjonalmuseet, which now nears its 2020 completion date. Sitting by the Rådhus, the new super-museum, a Kleihues + Schuwerk design that aims for 'longevity and dignity', will create a natural bridge between the new waterfront areas and the city centre.

☑ **Top Tips**

▶ Leave yourself enough time to see the entire collection rather than just snapping *The Scream* and leaving.

▶ Get in a visit before the gallery moves to its new modern home – the current neoclassical interiors are beautiful.

✕ **Take a Break**

Head to Fuglen (p119) for a bolstering pre-visit coffee and pastry or a post-*Scream* cocktail. If you fancy a beer, Røør (p44) is a block away.

JTB PHOTO/UIG VIA GETTY IMAGES ©

Top Sights
Akershus Festning

For seven centuries this imposing 13th-century fortress has been the city's most recognisable landmark, and still gives its glorious johnny-come-lately rivals, the Oslo Opera House and the Holmenkollen Ski Jump, a run for their scenic money. Akershus Festning (Akershus Fortress) is a wonderful place to imagine the city's early days, take in the view, or browse through one of its fascinating museums.

◉ Map p32, C6

admission free

🕑 6am-9pm

🚋 Christiania Square

The Fortress

When Oslo became Norway's capital in 1299, the threat of invading Swedes prompted King Håkon V to order the construction of a fortress. It was most notably the home of Margaret I of Denmark, the child bride of Håkon VI in 1363 and later ruler in her own right. Over the centuries it's been extended and modified many times, and was even struck by lightning, but traces of its medieval core survive. More than 60 buildings are scattered across the site; you could easily spend half a day exploring.

The Castle

The medieval facade of Akershus Slott (p36) hides a 17th-century palace within it. Built at the same time as Christian IV founded the modern Kristiania, it's a beautiful example of northern Renaissance style, with an exquisite castle chapel of pale painted panels and pale grey marble. The church contains the current royal family's mausoleum.

Norwegian Resistance Museum

Akershus Fortress was used by Nazi occupiers as a military base as well as a prison. Just next to a memorial to the resistance fighters who were executed here during the war is this fascinating and heartbreaking museum (p34). Dedicated to the active and very effective Norwegian resistance movement, it tells its important story through ephemera and objects as well as interpretative text.

Tour Time

Guided tours in Norwegian and English are conducted by enthusiastic young guides in period dress; their anecdotal accounts add a richness to a visit. There are two tour themes: one explores the construction of the fortress and its early military uses; the other explores the period when the fortress was known as Slaveriet (the slavery) and its 650 years of keeping prisoners in captivity. Both begin at the tourist centre's atmospheric 'red house'.

SAIKO3P/SHUTTERSTOCK ©

☑ Top Tips

▶ There's a daily musical guard parade at 1pm from May to September.

▶ If you believe in ghosts, have your ghost-radar at the ready.

▶ Horse-lovers can take a peek at the equine members of Oslo's police force here.

✖ Take a Break

Take coffee and cake at the Armed Forces Museum. Pretty vaulted cafe Grosch (p41) is just beyond the fortress walls.

Top Sights
Royal Palace

The Norwegian royal family's home since 1905, the Royal Palace (Det Kongelige Slott) must be one of the most accessible and laid-back of royal residences anywhere in the world. Come for a tour of its 19th-century rooms, a stroll around its walls or a loll in its rambling, lush parkland, the Slottsparken.

👁 Map p32, A3

☎ 81 53 31 33

www.royalcourt.no

Slottsparken 1

palace tours adult/child 135/105kr

🕑 guided tours noon, 2pm, 2.20pm & 4pm Jun–mid-Aug

🚊 Slottsparken

The Palace

Sitting on a rise known as Bellevue, at the top of Karl Johans gate, the pale-yellow stuccoed brick and pared-back neoclassical design of Norway's royal seat exude a dignified calm, free of bombast. State rooms reflect various eras from the building's 25-year construction period, including grand halls and ceremonial dining rooms. One of the prettiest is the Bird Room, still used as the king's waiting room. Dating to 1843, it reflects the National Romantic period and its cultivating of a love of nature and folk culture.

Slottsparken

One of Oslo's largest and earliest parks (p34) surrounds the palace, an extraordinarily lovely and surprisingly bucolic mix of lush grassy pastures and clusters of towering, majestic trees. Established at the same time as the palace, it's an appealing example of the Romantic ideal of the mid-19th century; it retains this effortless style today. Don't miss its three ponds, part of the original design.

Queen Sonja Art Stable

Modelled on those of Buckingham Palace, these former stables (p34) had been used as storage since WWII, and were opened to the public for the first time in 2017.

The Royals

The Palace was built at the Swedish-French Bernadotte monarch King Karl Johan's bidding, but was never occupied full time until Norwegian independence in 1905, when King Håkon VII, originally a Danish royal by the name of Prince Carl, was installed, along with his wife, the new Queen Maud. The current HM King Harald V is their grandson. The Norwegian royals are known for their down-to-earth sense of humour and liberal politics. They are also a family of keen hikers and sailors; the Queen is also a keen photographer and patron of the arts.

VISIONS OF OUR LAND/GETTY IMAGES ©

☑ Top Tips

▶ The changing of the guards happens daily at 9am.

▶ Summer tour tickets can be bought on the day, but they do reach capacity so pre-purchase at www.ticketmaster.no.

▶ The palace is the centre of the charming National Day children's marches on 17 May.

✕ Take a Break

Head to Kafe Oslo (p117) at the Litteraturhuset for lunch (a certain Crown Princess is said to be a fan). The raffish Kunstnernes Hus (p119) has great wine by the glass and does early-evening pizza.

Local Life
Bar-Hopping in the City Centre

The centre's compact size makes for an easy bar-hopping evening, with lots of changes of pace and mood. Locals often start the evening at home, pop into a few of their neighbourhood haunts and then head into the centre, so note that your night may get increasingly more raucous as it wears on.

① Sentralen

Depending on whether there's a concert (or a few) on, the fabulously refurbished old bank **Sentralen** (☑22 33 33 22; www.sentralen.no; Øvre Slottsgate 3; 🚇Øvre Slottsgate) can be either a cruisy place to begin your night or a fabulously hectic one. Grab a pizza or some Neo Nordic small plates here to line your stomach, have a drink at the beautiful hidden **Gullbaren** (Map p32, C5; www.sentralen.no/arrangement/gullbaren;

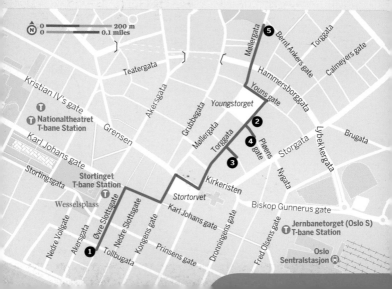

3rd fl, Øvre Slottsgate 3; ⊙check website for details; 🚊Øvre Slottsgate) and get ready to kick on.

❷ Youngstorget Pit Stop

Join the city's arty intellectuals and the odd politician at **Internasjonalen** (📞468 25 240; www.internasjonalen.no; Youngstorget 2; ⊙10am-1am Mon, to 3am Tue-Sat, 4pm-1am Sun; 🚊Brugata) and take in the iconic Folketeateret building – built in 1929 and both a theatre and headquarters of the Norwegian Labour Party – while sipping on a cocktail.

❸ Secret Passages

As the night wears on, swap cocktail swank for a little grunge, and head to this nondescript alleyway where you'll find the legendary **Angst** (http://angst bar.blogspot.com; Torggata 11; ⊙noon-11pm Mon & Tue, to 1.30am Wed & Thu, to 3am Fri & Sat, 2-11pm Sun; 🚊Brugata) bar and several other small bars where the beer

flows. If you're in need of a late-night snack, there's no shortage of hot dogs, burgers and tapas here, too.

❹ Bands & Beergarden

Oslo's rock-and-roll edge has long been celebrated at **Mono** (www.cafe mono.no; Pløens gate 4; ⊙4pm-3am; 🚊Brugata). Stay for a band or just do beers in the year-round courtyard under a portrait of Richard Hell, where you can talk up-and-coming Norwegian music with the locals.

❺ Last Drinks

Wander with the crowds towards Vulkan, where you'll find more and more bars and venues. No matter who's playing at dark and rambling **Revolver** (Map p86, A4; 📞22 20 22 32; www.revolver oslo.no; Møllergata 32; ⊙6pm-3.30am; 🚊Brugata), the front bar – a favourite with the city's music-industry crowd – is a great place to finish the night.

Oslo

Oslo Visitor Centre

Dronning Eufemias gate
Oslo Sentralstasjon
Operagata
Oslo Opera House
Strandgata
Prinsens gate
Fred Olsens gate
40
37
Skippergata
Tollbugata
Viking Biking
Kirkegata
Dronningens gate
Rådhusgata
11
Operatunnelen
Langkaia
Bjørvika
29
25
23
Bank Plassen
Myntgata
Nedre Slottsgate
20
Grev Wedels Plass
Glacisgata
Akershusstranda
Akershus Festning
Akershus Fortress
Information Centre
Akershus Slott
9
Kirkegata
Kongens gate
17
Norwegian Resistance Museum
4
Akershusstranda
Akershusvollen
Kontraskjæret
Rådhusgata

AKER BRYGGE
Rådhusbrygge
Standen
Bryggetorget
Bryggegata

Pipervika

Hovedøya

◉ Top Sights	p24
◎ Sights	p34
✕ Eating	p37
🍷 Drinking	p42
🎭 Entertainment	p44
🛍 Shopping	p45

N
0   0.2 miles
0   400 m

Sights

Ibsen Museet
MUSEUM

1 Map p32, A3

While downstairs houses a small and rather idiosyncratic museum, it's Ibsen's former apartment, which you'll need to join a tour to see, that is unmissable. This was the playwright's last residence and his study remains exactly as he left it, as does the bedroom where he uttered his famously enigmatic last words, *'Tvert imot!'* ('To the contrary!'), before dying on 23 May 1906. (Ibsen Museum; 📞40 02 36 30; www.ibsenmuseet.no; Henrik Ibsens Gate 26; adult/child 115/30kr; ⏰11am-6pm May-Sep, to 4pm Oct-Apr, guided tours hourly; 🚇Slottsparken)

Slottsparken
PARK

2 Map p32, B3

Rising up above the western end of central Oslo is the sloping parkland of Slottsparken, one of the capital's first public parks. Filled with rambling pastures, flowering meadows, a duck pond or three, and wooded arcades, it's a lovely place for a quiet walk and, despite its royal credentials (the Norwegian royal family's main residence sits at its apex), has a natural rather than stately beauty. (Slottsparken; admission free; ⏰24hr; 🚇Slottsparken)

Queen Sonja Art Stable
GALLERY

3 Map p32, A2

The former palace stables, used for half a century as storage, were reopened as a public gallery space by Queen Sonja on her 80th birthday. The charming 19th-century building hosts yearly exhibitions as well as a permanent collection of fascinating photographs both by and collected by the late Queen Maud (1869–1938). (Queen Sonja KunstStall; www.royalcourt.no; adult 100kr; ⏰11am-5pm Thu-Sun; 🚇Slottsparken)

Norwegian Resistance Museum
MUSEUM

4 Map p32, C6

Within the Akershus Fortress complex the Norwegian Resistance Museum stands adjacent to a memorial for resistance fighters executed on this spot during WWII. The small but worthwhile museum covers the dark years of German occupation, as well as the jubilant day of 9 May 1945 when peace was declared. Artefacts include

---

Q Local Life
Winter Wonderland

The most central, and romantic, ice skating in Oslo can be found at the **Spikersuppa** (Map p32, C4; Karl Johans gate; admission free; 🚇Øvre Slottsgate) outdoor ice rink, where you can skate for free whenever it's cold enough to freeze over (around November to March). The rink often closes at around 3pm to allow for ice preparation. Skates can be hired for 100kr.

M:PREMAGNUM/GETTY IMAGES ©

Oslo Cathedral

underground newspapers, numerous maps and photographs, and, most intriguingly, a set of dentures that belonged to a Norwegian prisoner of war in Poland that were wired to receive radio broadcasts. (Norges Hjemmefront Museet; 📞23 09 31 38; www.forsvarets museer.no; adult/child 60/30kr; ⏰10am-5pm Mon-Sat, from 11am Sun Jun-Aug, 10am-4pm Mon-Fri, from 11am Sat & Sun Sep-May; 🚋Christiania Square)

vi, vii   GALLERY

5 ◉ Map p32, B4

An independent gallery with a good reputation for interesting shows from up-and-coming artists, housed in an interesting 1930s building.

(📞906 75 993; www.vivii.no; Tordenskiolds gate 12; ⏰1-5pm Thu & Fri, noon-4pm Sat; 🚋Kontraskjæret)

Oslo Cathedral   CATHEDRAL

6 ◉ Map p32, D4

The highlights of a visit to Oslo Cathedral, which dates from 1697, are the elaborate stained-glass windows by Emanuel Vigeland (brother of Gustav) and the painted ceiling, completed between 1936 and 1950. The exceptional altarpiece, a 1748 model of *The Last Supper and the Crucifixion* by Michael Rasch, was an original feature of the church (from 1700), but it was moved all over the country before being returned from Prestnes church in

Understand
Old Oslo, Modern Christiania

As much as it might still rile, it was the Danish King Christian IV who was responsible for the Oslo we know today. Christian chose to rebuild the city below the Akershus Fortress so it could be more easily defended, and, in the spirit of (late) Renaissance order, it was to form a rectangular grid. This town planning (and some of the exquisite 17th-century streetscapes) can still be seen today in the area known as Kvadraturen (the quad) between the Akershus Fortress and Oslo Cathedral, Øvre Vollgate and Skippergata. The king, in an early act of Danish brand management, renamed the new modern city Christiania. It wasn't until 1925 that Christiania again became Oslo.

Majorstue in 1950. (Domkirke; Stortorvet 1; admission free; ⏰24hr; Stortorvet)

Historisk Museum
MUSEUM

7 Map p32, B3

The Historical Museum is actually three museums under one roof. Most interesting is the ground-floor **National Antiquities Collection** (Oldsaksamlingen), which has displays of Viking-era coins, jewellery and ornaments, and includes the only complete Viking helmet ever found. Look out for the 9th-century **Hoen**

treasure (2.5kg), the largest such find in Scandinavia. A section on medieval religious art includes the doors and richly painted ceiling of the Ål stave church (built around 1300). (📞22 85 19 00; www.khm.uio.no; Frederiks gate 2, University of Oslo; adult/child 50kr/free, includes entrance to Vikingskipmuseet; ⏰10am-5pm Tue-Sun; Tullinløkka)

Rådhus
ARCHITECTURE

8 Map p32, B4

This twin-towered town hall, completed in 1950 to commemorate Oslo's 900th anniversary, houses the city's political administration and is filled with mid-century tributes to Norwegian cultural and working life. Something of an Oslo landmark, the bombast of its red-brick functionalist exterior is polarising, if unmissable. It's here that the Nobel Peace Prize is awarded on 10 December each year. (Fridtjof Nansens plass; admission free; ⏰9am-6pm, guided tours 10am, noon & 2pm Jun–mid-Jul; Kontraskjæret)

Akershus Slott
CASTLE

9 Map p32, C6

In the 17th century Christian IV renovated Akershus Castle into a Renaissance palace, although the front remains decidedly medieval. In its dungeons you'll find dark cubbyholes where outcast nobles were kept under lock and key, while the upper floors contained sharply contrasting lavish banquet halls and staterooms. (Akershus Castle; 📞22 41 25 21; www.nasjonalefestningsverk.no; Kongens

gate; adult/child 60/30kr, with Oslo Pass
free; ⏰11am-4pm Mon-Sat, noon-5pm Sun;
🚊Christiania Square)

Parliament Building

NOTABLE BUILDING

10 👁 Map p32, C4

Built in 1866, Norway's yellow-brick
parliament building is one of Europe's
more charming parliaments. If you
find yourself really hooked on Norwegian political debate, you can tune into
the live action through the Stortinget
website. (Stortinget; 📞23 31 33 33; www.
stortinget.no; Karl Johans gate 22; admission
free; ⏰guided tours in English 10am & 1pm Jul
& Aug, Sat rest of year; 🚊Øvre Slottsgate)

Viking Biking

CYCLING

11 👁 Map p32, C5

This excellent outfit is a great place to
head if you want to explore Oslo on
two wheels. It runs a range of guided
bike tours, including a three-hour
'City Highlights' route through some
of Oslo's parks and backstreets, plus
a 'River Tour' along the path beside
the Akerselva River, both designed to
avoid traffic wherever possible. (📞412
66 496; www.vikingbikingoslo.com; Nedre
Slottsgate 4; 3hr tour adult/child 350/200kr;
⏰9.30am-6pm; 🚊Øvre Slottsgate)

Oslo Promenade

WALKING

12 👁 Map p32, B4

Oslo Guide Service conducts a 1½-
hour evening city walk starting from
in front of the Rådhus (town hall) at
5.30pm; no booking required. The
guides are knowledgeable and enter-
taining, making this a good option
for getting an insider's view of Oslo.
They also offer personalised city tours
for groups of 10 or more, which have
to be booked in advance. (📞22 42 70
20; www.guideservice.no; adult/child 200kr/
free, with Oslo Pass free; ⏰end May-Sep;
🚊Rådhusplassen)

Eating

Sentralen Restaurant

NEW NORDIC €€

13 🍴 Map p32, C4

One of Oslo's best dining experiences
is also its most relaxed. A large dining
room with a bustling open kitchen,
filled with old social club chairs
and painted in tones of deep, earthy
green, draws city workers, visitors and
natural-wine-obsessed locals in equal
measure. Small-plate dining makes it
easy to sample across the appealing
Neo Nordic menu. (📞22 33 33 22; www.
sentralen.no; Øvre Slottsgate 3; small plates
85-195kr; ⏰11am-10pm Mon-Sat; 🚊Øvre
Slottsgate)

Grand Café

NORWEGIAN €€

14 🍴 Map p32, C4

At 11am sharp, Henrik Ibsen would
leave his apartment and walk to
Grand Café for a lunch of herring,
beer and one shot of aquavit (an
alcoholic drink made from potatoes
and caraway liquor). His table is still

Understand
Art Capital

Something of an insider's secret, Oslo's art scene is egalitarian, flush with cash, vibrant, erudite, unpretentious and often fearless. Contemporary collections are full of heavy-hitting international names (and ridiculously uncrowded) and there's a flourishing, fun artist-run scene (which you'll often find happily full of crowds of young artists).

The Big Collections

With the Museet for Samtidskunst in storage until 2020, Oslo's contemporary must-sees are both private concerns. The collection at Astrup Fearnley Museet (p52) is particularly strong in American conceptual and photographic art, with significant pieces by European and Norwegian artists too. It's home to the stratospherically expensive Jeff Koons' *Michael Jackson and Bubbles*. Ekebergparken (p107) has 26 hectares of pasture, forest and rocky outcrops that are dotted with the idiosyncratic sculpture collection of a local property developer. Its 37 works include Jenny Holzer's hidden up winding tracks, a gleefully menacing Jake and Dinos Chapman, a huge Louise Bourgeois hanging from towering trees, a sublime underground chamber care of James Turrell and a sunny yellow Sarah Lucas standing erect as a welcoming sentinel.

Commercial Gallery Scene

Norwegian art stars such as Matias Faldbakken, Sverre Bjertnæs and the now New York–based Bjarne Melgaard show at a handful of leading commercial galleries that are seldom preoccupied by what collectors want (there aren't that many), instead often favouring the provocative over market-driven art trends. Leading the pack are Standard Oslo (p87) and Rod Bianco (p85) – both located in a nondescript stretch of road in between Grünerløkka and St Hanshaugen, with Rod Bianco insouciantly hidden up an unmarked staircase next to a mechanic's workshop. Both show the country's best mid-career artists: expect highly conceptual work.

Independent & Artist-Run Galleries

Because of the generous support artists in Norway receive and the strength of the visual art program at Oslo National Academy of the Arts (KHiO), there is also an incredibly vibrant artist-run space scene. These include Kunsthall Oslo (p121); spaces such as 1857 (p105) and vi, vii (p35), which have both international connections and reputations; and nyMusikk (p108), which hosts new music and sound art shows.

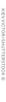

Rådhus (p36)

here. Don't worry, though, today you can take your pick from perfectly plated, elegantly sauced cod and mussels, spelt risotto with mushrooms or cured lamb and potato. (☏23 21 20 18; www.grand.no; Karl Johans gate 31; mains 145-295kr; ☺11am-11pm Mon-Fri, from noon Sat, noon-9pm Sun; ⓜStortinget)

Sentralen Cafeteria
CAFE, PIZZA €

 15 Map p32, C4

At the heart of the Sentralen complex, this day-to-evening place really is a cafeteria for the area's many freelancers and creative industry workers. Join them for a morning coffee and pastry or sandwich (both care of the

Handwerk bakery), eat in or take away healthy lunch dishes or stay for wood-fired sourdough pizza and beer from 4pm on weekdays or from noon on weekends. (☏22 33 33 22; Akersgata 2; meals 90-160kr; ☺7.30am-midnight Mon-Fri, from 10am Sat, 11am-5pm Sun; ⓜØvre Slottsgate)

Fiskeriet
SEAFOOD €€

16 Map p32, E3

You'd be forgiven for thinking that you're actually dining in a fish shop, as this seafood-serving powerhouse is also one of Oslo's best places to pick up market-fresh produce. And, yes, it makes for a fun and atmospheric lunch or dinner. The menu is delightfully predictable with fish and chips, traditional fish soup, Mediterranean-style *baccala* (salt cod), seafood casserole and fish cakes. (📞22 42 45 40; http://fiskeriet.com; Youngstorget 2; mains 165-249kr; 🕙11am-9pm Mon-Fri, from noon Sat, noon-8pm Sun, shop 10am-6pm Mon-Sat; 🚇Brugata)

Solsiden   SEAFOOD €€€

 17 🍴 Map p32, B5

Nestled beneath Oslo's fortress, looking out to Aker Brygge, Solsiden serves up some of the city's best-loved seafood dishes in an old warehouse that's airy and atmospheric (and a maritime-kitsch-free zone). You can do simple shell-on shrimps by the half-kilo (265kr) or really go to town with a platter of lobster, shrimps, scallops, snow crab, mussels and crayfish (755kr per person). (📞22 33 36 30; www.solsiden.no; Søndre Akershus Kai 34; mains 295-315kr; 🕙4.30-10pm Mon-Sat, to 9pm Sun; 🚇Kontraskjæret)

Illegal Burgers   BURGERS €

 18 🍴 Map p32, D3

Well-priced burgers with large char-grilled patties, interesting gourmet variations and chunky fries. (📞22 20 33 02; Møllergata 23; burgers 96-142kr; 🕙2-11pm Mon-Thu, to 1am Fri & Sat; 🚇37)

Justisen   NORWEGIAN, BURGERS €€

 19 🍴 Map p32, D3

A pubby people-pleaser, this incredibly charming and atmospheric place dates back to 1820. There's a large

---

Understand
Norwegian Romantic Artists

The rebirth of Norwegian identity with the new constitution of 1814 saw a blossoming of artistic production. The Nasjonalgalleriet's large national collection is a great way to discover this fascinating moment in history. Johan Christian Dahl is represented by 147 paintings and 1500 works on paper alone, and there are many works by Thomas Fearnley and Peder Balke too. The amount of work on show can be overwhelming, but stay with it. There's both a simple joy in recognising many of the iconic Norwegian destinations in the west coast, the Arctic and the centre, and gaining an understanding of the national psyche. Don't miss the much-loved *Bridal Procession on the Hardangerfjord* by Adolph Tidemand and Hans Gude, a painting that speaks to Norwegians across the centuries. If you're visiting the Royal Palace, take note of the giddily pretty Bird Room. Designed in 1843 by painter Johannes Flintoe, it's another example of the explosion of interest in Norway's natural beauty and its history. The murals are filled with unique local birdlife, while dragon motifs and other decoration conjure traditional stave churches.

Norwegian menu to try, but you can't beat the happy-hour burger and drink deal for 255kr, especially if enjoyed in the all-weather beer garden. (☑22 42 24 72; www.justisen.no; Møllergata 15; mains 135-240kr; ☒Brugata)

Grosch INTERNATIONAL €€

20 🍴 Map p32, C5

Located in the pretty surrounds of the Nasjonalmuseet's Arkitektur building, this museum cafe serves up burgers, tapas, soups, sandwiches and sweet things. Count on Scandinavian designer chairs too. (☑22 42 12 12; www.groschbistro.no; Bankplassen 3; lunch dishes 95-165kr; ☺11am-5pm Mon-Wed & Fri, to 7pm Thu, noon-5pm Sat & Sun; ☒Øvre Slottsgate)

Miss Sophie EUROPEAN €€

21 🍴 Map p32, A3

A pretty corner shop opposite the park does all-day dining in glamorous surrounds. There are simple, if rather luxurious, pan-European standards such as steak frites, rösti done with sweet potato, or pasta with truffles on offer, although the super-popular weekend brunch is less so, with omelettes vying for attention with more Instagram-friendly dishes such as chia pudding, pancakes, banana bread and eggs Benedict. (☑21 09 78 79; www.misssophierestaurant.no; Henrik Ibsens gate 4; mains 175-275kr, brunch dishes 65-175kr; ☺5pm-1am Tue-Fri, noon-2am Sat, to 6pm Sun; ☒Slottsparken)

Theatercafeen NORWEGIAN €€€

22 🍴 Map p32, B4

A favourite with Norwegian families during Christmas and on 17 May (Constitution Day), the Theatercafeen, located directly across from the National Theatre, presents Norwegian classics in Viennese surroundings that have been wowing diners since 1900. The menu conjures Norway's wild and stormy seas and its dark forests, and delivers them up in dishes such as turbot with caviar cream, and halibut with asparagus and mushrooms. (☑22 82 40 50; Stortingsgata 24/26; mains 229-380kr; ☺noon-11pm Mon-Sat, 3-10pm Sun; ☒Nationaltheatret)

Café Skansen MEDITERRANEAN €€€

23 🍴 Map p32, C5

Café Skansen's dark wood and tiled dining room makes for an atmospheric change from Aker Brygge's stringent contemporary architecture and the menu here is in keeping with its surrounds, with lots of traditional seafood dishes, lamb and steaks. The Danish sausages with red wine gravy are a great 4pm dinner if you've been out exploring the Oslofjord and are in need of some warming sustenance. (☑24 20 13 11; www.cafeskansen.no; Rådhusgata 32; mains 205-248kr; ☺11am-midnight Mon-Fri, noon-midnight Sat, noon-11pm Sun; ☒Kontraskjæret)

Kaffebrenneriet
CAFE €

24 ✖ Map p32, C3

Opposite the National Gallery, this relaxed branch of one of Norway's best cafe chains has good espresso and filter coffee, packets of coffee to take away, pastries and a good selection of filled rolls. (www.kaffebrenneriet.no; Universtetsgata 1; snacks 35-105kr; ⏱7am-7pm Mon-Fri, 9am-6pm Sat & Sun; 🚊Tullinløkka)

People & Coffee
INTERNATIONAL €

25 ✖ Map p32, C5

A cafe that is also a nice lunch spot with Latin American, African and Asian dishes popping up alongside carrot cake, soup and coffee. Coffee beans are sourced from fair-trade suppliers. (☎906 02 510; www.peopleand coffee.no; Rådhusgata 21; mains 79-149kr; ⏱7am-6pm; 🚊Christiania Square)

Q Local Life
Summer Rooftops

Not just for hotel guests, or tourists, the downtown **Grims Grenka** (Map p35 C5; ☎23 10 72 00; www. firsthotels.no; Kongens gate 5; s/d 1350/1500kr; P❄🛜; T Kongens gate) has a summer terrace bar with great views, as does the **Grand Hotel** (Map p32, C4; ☎23 21 20 00; www.grand.no; Karl Johans gate 31; d 1890-2800kr; P🛜🚲; T Stortinget), which is open all year.

Elias Mat & Sånt
BISTRO €€

26 ✖ Map p32, C3

A good bet for simple dishes in the city centre, and dead handy after a jaunt around the National Gallery. Tempting traditional options include pollack fish fillet with baby potatoes, or rich reindeer stew with a brown cheese sauce and mashed potatoes, served in a cosy little space. Lunch dishes such as fish soup or mussels are good value. (☎22 20 22 21; www. cafeelias.no; Kristian Augusts gate 14; lunch mains 109-179kr, dinner mains 184-269kr; ⏱5-11pm Sun & Mon, from 11am Tue-Sat; 🚊Tullinløkka)

Ruffino Ristorante
ITALIAN €€€

27 ✖ Map p32, A3

An upmarket, traditional place where locals go to eat Italian standards including a large range of housemade pasta and seafood dishes. As befits such a family-friendly place, it's happy to do half-serves for kids. (☎22 55 32 80; www.ruffino.no; Arbins gate 1; pasta 170-199kr, mains 300kr; ⏱4-11pm Mon-Sat; 🚊Slottsparken)

Drinking

Kulturhuset
BAR, PUB

28 🍺 Map p32, E3

The Norwegian notion of culture being an interactive, collective enterprise combines here with their

IZZET KERIBAR/GETTY IMAGES ©

Theatercafeen (p41)

exceptional ability to have a good time. The city's 'culture house' moved into this beautiful, rambling old four-storey building in 2017, but it feels as if it's been part of the Oslo fabric for years. (http://kulturhusetioslo.no; Youngs gate 6; ⏰8am-3.30am Mon-Fri, from 11am Sat & Sun; 🚇Brugata)

Gullbaren BAR

29 🚇 Map p32, C5

Hidden at the top of the grand marble staircase in the original bank section of Sentralen, and decorated with found objects from the pre-renovation bank headquarters, this tiny bar may just be Oslo's most atmospheric. (www.sentralen.no/arrangement/gullbaren;

3rd fl, Øvre Slottsgate 3; ⏰check website for details; 🚇Øvre Slottsgate)

Himkok COCKTAIL BAR, BEER GARDEN

30 🚇 Map p32, E3

First things first: the door is unmarked, save for a small, decorative 'H'. Also good to know: the crew behind Himkok are the inventors of the 'taptail' – quality cocktails on tap. This also happens to be a distillery, so the vodka and gin in your expertly mixed drink has been made on the premises. (🖉22 42 22 02; www.facebook.com/HIMKOK.OSLO; Storgata 27; ⏰5pm-3am Sun-Wed, from 3pm Thu-Sat; 🚇Brugata)

Top Tip
Secret Strøget
Strøget passage (Map p32, E3), running between Torggata and Storgata, is like a grunge shopping mall, with a fantastic collection of bars and casual restaurants lined up in a row and hidden from street view at either end.

Oslo Camping

BAR

31　Map p32, D3

Norwegians like to have a pub activity on hand for those potentially awkward moments before the social lubrication kicks in. Here the activity is an 18-hole minigolf course. Cheap beer, metal clubs and small hard balls – what could go wrong? Nothing in fact, with lots of happy, minigolfing fun to be had, DJs on weekends and toast if you're hungry. (http://oslo-camping.no; Møllergata 12; minigolf 105kr; 1pm-1am Mon-Thu, to 3am Fri & Sat, to midnight Sun; Brugata)

Røør

BEER HALL

32　Map p32, C5

Craft-beer credentials (check out that blackboard list!) meet Norwegian fun with shuffleboard, an excellent vinyl collection and vending-machine snacks over two floors. There's around 70 beers on tap alone and a not-so-shabby selection of ciders and wine by the glass too. (Rosenkrantz gate 4; 1pm-3am; Tinghuset)

Sosialen

PUB

33　Map p32, D3

A good choice if you're not sure if you want to go out for a drink or have something to eat and kick on. There's a menu of Norwegian and international favourites to be had in the nicely industrial front room, or stay on for drinks and DJs. (22 41 50 06; http://sosialen.com; Møllergata 13; 4pm-midnight Mon & Tue, to 2am Wed & Thu, 3pm-3.30am Fri & Sat; Stortinget)

Stockfleths

CAFE

34　Map p32, C4

Founded in 1895, the award-winning Stockfleths is one of Oslo's oldest coffee shops. It also serves wholegrain bread with brown cheese, pastries and smoothies. (www.stockfleths.as; Lille Grensen; 7am-6pm Mon-Fri, 10am-5pm Sat; Stortinget)

Entertainment

Nationaltheatret

THEATRE

35　Map p32, B3

Norway's showcase theatre, with its lavish hall, was constructed specifically as a venue for the works of Norwegian playwright Henrik Ibsen, whose works are still performed here. Its historicist style dates from 1899 and is care of Oslo's Henrik Bull. (National Theatre; www.nationaltheatret.no; Stortingsgata 15; tickets 160-480kr; Nationaltheatret)

Nationaltheatret

Saga Kino

CINEMA

36 Map p32, B3

The six-screen Saga Kino cinema shows first-run movies, including Hollywood fare, in their original language; the entrance is on Olav V's gate. (22 83 23 75; www.oslokino.no; Stortingsgata 28; Nationaltheatret)

Shopping

Norwegian Rain

FASHION & ACCESSORIES

37 Map p32, D5

Bergen comes to Oslo! This west coast design superstar creates what might be the world's most covetable

raincoats. This Oslo outpost stocks the complete range as well as creative director T-Michael's woollen suits, detachable-collar shirts, leather shoes and bags, not to mention limited editions of Kings of Convenience LPs. (996 03 411; http://norwegianrain.com; Kirkegata 20; 10am-6pm Mon-Fri, to 5pm Sat; Nationaltheatret)

Tronsmo

BOOKS

38 Map p32, C3

A social hub as much as a bookshop, come for its large range of English-language books and stay for a reading or performance. There's a large LGBT section and a basement full of comics and graphic novels. (22 99 03 99; www.

tronsmo.no; Universitetsgata 12; ⊘9am-5pm Mon-Wed, to 6pm Thu & Fri, 10am-4pm Sat; 🚇Tullinløkka)

FWSS FASHION & ACCESSORIES

39 🔒 Map p32, C4

New flagship of this fast-growing Norwegian label, known for its easy basics as well as seasonal collections that combine Scandinavian simplicity with a pretty, playful edge. (Fall Winter Spring Summer; http://fallwinterspringsummer.com; Prinsens gate 22; ⊘10am-7pm Mon-Fri, to 6pm Sat; 🚇Øvre Slottsgate)

Tom Wood FASHION & ACCESSORIES

40 🔒 Map p32, D5

Oslo label Tom Wood's restrained monochromatic clothes are as Norwegian as you'll get, with their austere simplicity and high-quality natural materials. The silver jewellery will please fans of 20th-century Scandinavian design too.

Local Life
The Fashion Quad

Head to the **Kvadraturen** (Map p33, C5) – Nedre Slottsgate, Kirkegata and Prinsens gate in particular – for the city centre's most interesting shops. This fashion-forward zone takes in Promenaden, a new upmarket fashion district, where Scandinavian designers such as Filipa K, Marimekko, Norwegian Rain, FWSS and Acne Studio mix with the usual international luxury labels.

(📞919 06 226; http://tomwoodproject.com; Kirkegata 20; ⊘11am-6pm Mon-Fri, 10am-4pm Sat; 🚇Dronningens gate)

Råkk og Rålls MUSIC

41 🔒 Map p32, C4

Crate-digger heaven: a huge, rambling den of secondhand vinyl, mostly from the '70s and '80s, and much else besides. (📞22 41 17 01; Stortingsgata 8; ⊘11am-6pm Mon-Sat; 🚇Stortinget)

Oslo Kunsthandel ART

42 🔒 Map p32, C3

Whether you're in the market for museum-quality Modernist paintings and stunning mid-century furniture or not, this commercial gallery is a fabulous browse. It hosts good shows of emerging Norwegian artists at the front, while its resale pieces fill the rest of the large industrial space. These also include silver, glass, ceramics and rustic pieces as well as the previously mentioned modernist icons. (📞22 60 80 10; http://oslokunsthandel.no; Kristian Augusts gate 13; ⊘11am-5pm Tue-Fri, noon-4pm Sat & Sun; 🚇Tullinløkka)

Glasmagasinet Department Store DEPARTMENT STORE

43 🔒 Map p32, D4

This iconic city department store dates back to 1899 and has a good range of Scandinavian brands you know you want. (www.glasmagasinet.no; Stortorvet 9; ⊘10am-7pm Mon-Fri, to 6pm Sat; 🚇Stortorvet)

Café Skansen (p41)

Norli

BOOKS

44 Map p32, C3

The largest bookshop in Norway stocks a good range of foreign-language titles as well as numerous travel guides and maps. (www.norli.no; Universitetsgata 20-24; ⏲10am-7pm Mon-Sat; 🚃Nationaltheatret)

Norway Designs

FASHION & ACCESSORIES

45 Map p32, B3

Features designer clothing and beautiful glassware, stationery and watches within a stone's throw of the National Theatre. (www.norwaydesigns.no; Stortingsgata 28; ⏲10am-6pm Mon-Wed & Fri, to 7pm Thu, to 4pm Sat; 🚃Nationaltheatret)

Top Sights
Oslo Opera House

Getting There

🚶 Oslo Opera House is a short walk from Central Station.

Ⓣ Sentralstasjonen

Designed by Oslo-based architectural firm Snøhetta and costing around €500 million, Oslo's Opera House (Den Norske Opera & Ballett) resembles a glacier floating in the Bjørvika inlet. It is the city's most iconic building, a truly engaging piece of Scandinavian design that is inclusive, sensual and fun, whether you're an opera or ballet fan or not.

Design Savvy

Snøhetta's design incorporates a number of distinct elements: the interior 'wave wall'; the roof, known as the 'carpet'; and the 'factory', the functional workplace of the ballet and opera companies. Purposefully low slung to ensure it links with the city both visually and practically, the building asserts its social function as much as its sculptural one. It's a structure that also prompts questions about the relationship between city and fjord, Norway and the world, performance and quotidian life, artists and audience.

The Roof

Both prime selfie-zone and joyful place to wander, sprawl, laugh or think, the roof – a broad, etched and variegated expanse of luminous marble – fantastically encapsulates an essentially Norwegian notion of monumentality, the grandeur of which is horizontal and all-encompassing rather than vertical. It's an incredibly crafted piece of work too, engaging in both its close detail as well as its sheer size.

The Interior

The building's entrance is purposely small and unimposing, which adds to the sense of vastness that greets visitors on entering the main foyer. The windows alone are 15m high, flooding the foyer with light. The dominating feature is the 'wave wall'; made of a complex arrangement of golden oak cone curving up through the centre of the foyer, it provides access to the upper levels of the building while symbolically evoking a threshold.

Arts Factory

The multilevel workshops and offices of the several hundred opera and ballet workers are an integral and visible part of the building's design. The backstage craft that goes into a production is fascinating to see, and is consciously on show as a reminder of the collaborative nature of performances.

JOHN FREEMAN/GETTY IMAGES ©

👁 Map p33, E6

📞 21 42 21 21

www.operaen.no

Kirsten Flagstads plass 1

foyer free

🕐 foyer 10am-9pm Mon-Fri, 11am-9pm Sat, noon-9pm Sun

☑ Top Tips

▶ Guided **tours** (adult/child 100/60kr; 🕐 11am, noon & 1pm daily Jul-early Aug, 11am, noon & 1pm Mon-Fri, noon & 1pm Sat, 1pm Sun early Aug-31 Aug, 1pm Sun-Fri, noon Sat rest of year) take you into some of the building's 1100 rooms.

▶ Catch a performance for 100kr with a standing-room ticket.

✕ Take a Break

Sanguine Brasserie & Bar (mains 205-305kr, 2-/3-/4-course menu 410/525/585kr; 🕐 11am-9pm Mon-Sat, noon-8pm Sun) has elegant, casual meals.

Classic Norwegian food at Olympen (p110) on Grønland's Grønlandsleiret is just over the railway tracks.

Explore

Aker Brygge & Bygdøy

Join the sunny-day crowds at Aker Brygge and its island tip, Tjuvholmen ('Thief Island'), for a salt-air stroll, meal and a hit of contemporary architecture. You'll also find a couple of the city's best museums here. Further west, and best accessed by ferry, pretty, residential and rural-feeling Bygdøy is home to the city's most fascinating, and quintessentially Norwegian, museums.

OJ.MOREN/GETTY IMAGES ©

The Sights in a Day

☼ Head out to Bygdøy Peninsula by boat and start your day with a visit to the **Vikingskipshuset** (p54) and marvel at the sheer beauty of the more-than-900-year-old Viking vessels. Head to the **Norsk Folkemuseum** (p58) next and explore centuries of everyday Norwegian life and different eras of vernacular architecture spread out over a beautiful park.

☼ The semi-rural peninsula is a great place to wander between sights or you can ferry hop between them. Get your sea legs on at the **Norwegian Maritime Museum** (p58), where you can explore all things seafaring. Then head to **Vingen** (p60) for lunch after your return.

☾ Back at Akker Brygge, head up to the **Astrup Fearnley Museet** (p52) and its collection of international contemporary art that includes work by Jeff Koons, Cindy Sherman, Tom Sachs and Damien Hirst. Then wander the **Tjuvholmen Sculpture Park** (p57) outside and discover more incredible contemporary sculpture, before a quick visit to the **Nobels Fredssenter** (p57) and a seafood dinner at **Pipervika** (p60).

 **Top Sights**

Astrup Fearnley Museet (p52)

Vikingskipshuset (p54)

♥ **Best of Oslo**

Eating
Vingen (p60)

Architecture
Astrup Fearnley Museet (p52)

Museums
Astrup Fearnley Museet (p52)

Vikingskipshuset (p54)

Norwegian Maritime Museum (p58)

Getting There

🚋 **Tram** 12 runs right to Akker Brygge.

⚓ **Ferry** 91 makes the 15-minute run to Bygdøy every 20 to 30 minutes, leaving from Rådhusbrygge 3 – the pier opposite the Rådhus – and stopping at both Dronningen and Bygdøynes wharves.

🚌 **Bus** 21 runs to Akker Brygge from Grünerlokka via St Hanshaugen and lower Frogner.

Top Sights
Astrup Fearnley Museet

In a hilarious piece of high Norwegian irony, the capital's most high-profile contemporary art museum is not an oil-money-flush government-bolstered institution but a private foundation. Set in an impossibly beautiful site, the Astrup Fearnley Museet can't fail to amaze with a collection that shocks, entertains and inspires, and temporary shows that reflect the Norwegian and international zeitgeist.

◉ Map p56, D3

☎ 22 93 60 60

www.afmuseet.no

Strandpromenaden 2

adult/child 120kr/free

🕑 noon-5pm Tue, Wed & Fri, to 7pm Thu, 11am-5pm Sat & Sun

🚊 Aker brygge

The Building

Taking up the tip of Tjuvholmen island, Renzo Piano's €90-million, 7000-sq-metre building cleverly unites three separate structures with a dramatic, sail-like glass roof, its steel frame resembling ships' rigging, while the buildings themselves are clad in ever-silvering wood. Within there's a combination of monumental white cube spaces and more intimate sections. Some are entirely internal, others cut through by views to the sky or the Oslofjord.

The Americans

The Thomas Fearnley Foundation has, from the 1960s, amassed the country's most significant collection of postwar American art including a large number of conceptual sculpture and photographic works. While they've certainly branched out of late, the museum remains particularly strong in this field with the likes of Jeff Koons, Richard Prince, Cindy Sherman, Matthew Barney, Tom Sachs and Dan Colen well represented.

The Germans

No great contemporary art museum would be complete without an Anselm Kiefer, and the Astrup Fearnley has a couple of great ones. The chunky *Barren Landscape* sits next to *The High Priestess/Zweistromland*, a heavy work both metaphorically and physically (it's made of lead). Alongside these are Sigmar Polke's *Apparizione 1-3*, an important and exquisitely unworldly work.

New & Temporary Work

The museum aims to build dialogue between Norway and the international scene, and newer acquisitions and an exciting program of temporary shows reflect this. Works by Brazilian, Japanese, Chinese and Indian contemporary artists are worth seeking out, along with both emerging Norwegian artists and those who are prominent internationally, including Bjarne Melgaard and Matias Faldbakken.

CINEMATOGRAPHER/SHUTTERSTOCK ©

☑ Top Tips

▶ The Oslofjord views from the upstairs Kiefer and Polke room are breathtaking.

▶ If it's hot, bring your bikini for a quick dip at Tjuvholmen City Beach.

✕ Take a Break

Light and lovely Vingen (p60) does great coffee, smart lunches, wine and cocktails. Head across the bridge to Ling Ling (p61) for small Chinese dishes.

Top Sights
Vikingskipshuset

Prepare yourself for one of the most affecting historical experiences of your life at this museum. Three Viking ships – two in impossibly pristine condition – sit proudly in a light, purpose-built hall from the 1930s. Their dignified, dark presence makes the life of the much-mythologised Vikings seem vividly present.

◉ Map p56, A3

☏ 22 13 52 80

www.khm.uio.no

Huk Aveny 35

adult/child 80kr/free

⊙ 9am-6pm May-Sep, 10am-4pm Oct-Apr

🚌 91

Viking Life

Each of the ships on display were used as the centrepiece of massive burial sites. This means that not only the vessels were preserved, but also all the things a Viking might like to take with them to Valhalla. This great archaeological gift tells us much about Viking life, from nautical engineering capabilities, seacraft, and mercantile and military ambition, and gives a snapshot of a high-ranking citizen's everyday tastes and spiritual life.

The Ships

The three ships on display each have their own fascinating archaeological history. The *Oseberg* was discovered in 1903 and is undoubtedly the museum's most beautiful ship. Dating to 820, it's richly decorated from right below the waterline to its elegant serpent's-head prow. It was most likely a ceremonial ship rather than an ocean-going work vessel, although it has ample space for 30 oarsmen. Gazing up towards the prow from below is sure to give you goosebumps. The fast and flexible *Gokstad* dates to 890 and was found with most of its hull intact. Equipped for sail as well as rowing, it would have had a crew of around 34 Vikings and it remains a sleek and rather intimidating sight today. The smaller *Tune* was built in 910. A fast and sturdy vessel, it was intended either to move people (including slaves) or transport light, high-value cargo such as fur and glass, and was built to resist reasonably large waves.

The Bounty

Displayed in the hall's transepts are the stunning collections that were found in the burial chambers of the ships. Along with bodies of the dead Vikings, this comprised a huge and often surprising (eg peacock skeletons) array of things. One of the most significant is the *Oseberg* cart. Richly carved, this likely ceremonial vehicle pre-dates the ship and yielded four extraordinary carved animal heads and the skeletons of two Viking women.

TRABANTOS/SHUTTERSTOCK ©

☑ Top Tips

▶ Screened on the museum wall, the compelling and touching film *The Vikings Alive* is worth waiting to see.

▶ Make sure you head up the stairs to one of the small viewing nooks to get the full impact of the ship's decks.

▶ The museum shop not only does a turn in wooden swords, troll dolls and Viking hats, it has a great collection of Norwegian history and folklore titles too.

✗ Take a Break

There's a summertime kiosk in the museum courtyard for drinks and snacks.

Royal Palace
Slottsparken
Slottsplassen
Nationaltheatret
T-bane Station
7 Juni
Plass

Fridtjof
Nansens
plass

Nobels gate

Fredsenter Rådhusplassen

Oslo

City

Båtservice
Sightseeing

Radhusgata

Akershusstranda

Grundingen

Munkedamsveien

AKER
BRYGGE

Bryggegata

Stranden

Pipervika

Tjuvholmen
Sculpture Park

Holmens gate

Tjuvholmen

Astrup Fearnley
Museet

TJUVHOLMEN

Tjuvholmen
City Beach

Høvedøya

For reviews see

Top Sights   p52
Sights   p57
Eating   p60

500 m
0.25 miles

FREDERIK
Frederiks Gate

Slottsparken

Colbjørnsens
gate

SOLLIPLASS

Lokkeveien
Cort Adelers gate
Huitfeldts gate
Parkveien

Henrik Ibsens gate

Parkveien
Solli
plass

Niels Juels gate
Hydroparken
Thomles gate

Drammensveien

Munkedamsveien

Frognerstranda

Filipstadkaia

Filipstadveien

Vestheimgata
Frognerveien
Bygdøy alle

GIMLE

Sophus Lies gate
Frederik Stangs gate
Gabels gate
Svoldergata

Thomas Heftyes gate

Drammensveien

Frognerkilen

Niels Juels gate
Skovveien
Parkveien

FROGNER

Nobels gate

Frognerstranda

Museumsveien

Bygdøy allé

Bygdøy

Kon-Tiki
Museum

Fram
Museum

Polarship

Norwegian
Maritime
Museum

Bygdøynesveien

BYGDØY

Huk Aveny

Oscarshallveien
Museumsveien Dronning

Mellbakdalen

Løchenveien

Norsk
Folkemuseum

Vikingskipshuset

Wedels vei

Langviksveien

Nobels Fredssenter

Sights

Tjuvholmen Sculpture Park
SCULPTURE

 Map p56, D3

Like the Astrup Fearnley Museet that it surrounds, this sculpture park was designed by Renzo Piano and is also dedicated to international contemporary art. Don't miss Louise Bourgeois' magnificent and rather cheeky *Eyes* (1997), Ugo Rondinone's totemic and enchanting *Moonrise east. november* (2006) and Franz West's bright and tactile *Spalt* (2003). There are also works by Antony Gormley, Anish Kapoor, Ellsworth Kelly, and Peter Fischli and David Weiss. Along with the artwork there are canals and a small child-pleasing pebble beach. (http://afmuseet. no/en/om museet/skulpturparken; Tjuvholmen; admission free; ⏰24hr; 🚋Aker brygge)

Nobels Fredssenter
MUSEUM

 Map p56, E2

Norwegians take pride in their role as international peacemakers, and the Nobel Peace Prize is their gift to the men and women judged to have done the most to promote world peace over the course of the previous year. This state-of-the-art museum celebrates the lives and achievements of the winners with an array of digital displays that offer as much or as little information as you feel like taking in. (Nobel Peace

Top Tip
Ferry Tickets

Make sure you pre-buy your ferry ticket and get a return when you're heading out to Brygdøy – it's far cheaper.

Center; ☑48 30 10 00; www.nobelpeace center.org; Rådhusplassen 1; adult/student 100/65kr; ☺10am-6pm; 🚌Aker brygge)

Polarship Fram Museum
MUSEUM

 3 Map p56, B4

This museum is dedicated to one of the most enduring symbols of early polar exploration, the 39m schooner *Fram* (meaning 'Forward'). You can wander the decks, peek inside the cramped bunk rooms and imagine life at sea and among the polar ice. There are detailed exhibits complete with maps, pictures and artefacts of various expeditions, from Nansen's attempt to ski across the North Pole to Amundsen's discovery

Local Life
Waterfront Shopping

The streets behind the waterfront have a number of upmarket chain fashion shops favoured by local apartment dwellers. The Astrup Fearnley Museet has a well-stocked museum shop, with a interesting Norwegian design pieces, including jewellery, as well as furniture, books and magazines.

of the Northwest Passage. (Frammuseet; ☑23 28 29 50; www.frammuseum.no; Bygdøynesveien 36; adult/child 100/40kr, with Oslo Pass free; ☺9am-6pm Jun-Aug, 10am-5pm May & Sep, to 4pm Oct-May; 🚢91)

Norwegian Maritime Museum
MUSEUM

 4 Map p56, B4

Author Roald Dahl once said that in Norway everyone seems to have a boat, and the theory seems like quite a good one at the Norsk Maritime Museum. The museum depicts Norway's relationship with the sea, including the fishing and whaling industries, the seismic fleet (which searches for oil and gas), shipbuilding, wreck salvaging and pleasure craft. (www.mar museum.no; Bygdøynesveien 37; adult/child 100/30kr, with Oslo Pass free; ☺10am-5pm mid-May–Aug, to 4pm rest of year; 🚢91)

Norsk Folkemuseum
MUSEUM

5 Map p56, A3

This folk museum is Norway's largest open-air museum and one of Oslo's most popular attractions. The museum includes more than 140 buildings, mostly from the 17th and 18th centuries, gathered from around the country, rebuilt and organised according to region of origin. Paths wind past old barns, elevated *stabbur* (raised storehouses) and rough-timbered farmhouses with sod roofs sprouting wildflowers. Little people will be entertained by the numerous farm animals, horse and cart rides, and other activities. (Norwegian Folk Museum; ☎ 22 12 37 00; www.norskfolke museum.no; Museumsveien 10; adult/child 130/40kr, with Oslo Pass free; ⏱ 10am-6pm mid-May–mid-Sep, 11am-3pm Mon-Fri, 11am-4pm Sat & Sun mid-Sep–mid-May; 🚊 91)

Kon-Tiki Museum   MUSEUM

6 ◉ Map p56, B4

A favourite among children, this worthwhile museum is dedicated to the balsa raft *Kon-Tiki,* which Norwegian explorer Thor Heyerdahl sailed from Peru to Polynesia in 1947. The museum also displays the totora-reed boat *Ra II,* built by Aymara people on the Bolivian island of Suriqui in Lake Titicaca. Heyerdahl used it to cross the Atlantic in 1970. (☎ 23 08 67 67; www.kon-tiki.no; Bygdøynesveien 36; adult/child 100/40kr, with Oslo Pass free; ⏱ 9.30am-6pm Jun-Aug, 10am-5pm Mar-May, Sep & Oct, 10am-4pm Nov-Feb; 🚊 91)

Tjuvholmen City Beach   BEACH

7 ◉ Map p56, D3

Backed by a sprawling, lush and sculpture-dotted lawn, this tiny beach is often crowded with little Osloites splashing like there's no tomorrow, but it's still a delight. (Tjuvholmen; 🚊 Aker brygge)

Båtservice Sightseeing   BOATING

8 ◉ Map p56, E2

For a watery view of Oslo and the Oslofjord, Båtservice Sightseeing offers a whole array of tours aboard either a traditional wooden schooner or a more up-to-date motorboat. There's a hop-on, hop-off service from May to September (24-hour ticket 215kr). (☎ 23 35 68 90; www.boatsight seeing.com; Pier 3, Rådhusbrygge; per person 215-650kr; 🚊 Aker brygge)

Understand
Green, Clean, Car Free?

When the Labour Party, the Social Left and Greens romped to power in the city elections in 2015, they promised to ban private cars from the city centre by 2019, as part of a platform to slash greenhouse gas emissions and fight against climate change. But after a backlash by conservative politicians and concerned shopkeepers, the implementation of the plan has been rethought and its aims softened to a centre with 'the lowest possible private cars'.

Now, instead of an outright ban, it will be achieved via disincentives to motorists such as the removal of all city parking spaces, along with measures such as creating many kilometres of new bike lanes and investing heavily in further improving the public transport system, even though Oslo's is already one of the world's best. Still, the goal remains an ambitious one, and on track, with mass pedestrianisation of streets already happening.

Oslo City Train

SCENIC TRAIN

9 📍 Map p56, E2

Toot around central Oslo on one of two different 'trains'. Tours depart every half-hour from Aker Brygge and **University Square** on Karl Johans gate. Under fives are free. (📞48 17 99 99; www.oslocitytrain.no; adult/child 150/75kr; 🕐9.30am-5pm late Jun-Aug)

Eating

Vingen

NEW NORDIC €€

10 🍴 Map p56, D3

While honouring its role as museum cafe for Astrup Fearnley (p104) and a super-scenic pit stop, Vingen is so much more. Do drop in for excellent coffee, but also come for lunch or dinner with small, interesting

menus subtly themed in homage to the museum's current temporary show. Nightfall brings cocktails, and sometimes DJs and dancing in the museum lobby and, in summer, on the waterfront terrace. (📞901 51 595; http://vingenbar.no; Strandpromenaden 2; mains 145-240kr; 🕐10am-9pm Sun-Wed, to midnight Thu-Sat; 🚢Aker brygge)

Pipervika

SEAFOOD €€

11 🍴 Map p56, E2

If the weather is nice, nothing beats a shrimp lunch, with fresh shrimp on a baguette with mayonnaise and a spritz of lemon eaten dockside. The revamped fisherman's co-op still does takeaway peel-and-eat shrimp by the kilo, but you can now also relax with a sushi plate, oysters or a full seafood menu including fish burger on brioche or killer fish and chips. (www.pipervika.

Understand

Polar Explorer

Launched in 1892, the polar ship *Fram*, an unusually wide and shallow vessel and at the time the strongest ship ever built, spent much of its life trapped in the polar ice. From 1893 to 1896 Fridtjof Nansen's North Pole expedition took the schooner to Russia's New Siberian Islands, passing within a few degrees of the North Pole on their return trip to Norway. It was also used by Otto Sverdrup to travel to the Nunavut region of Canada, an Arctic archipelago west of Greenland, during 1898 to 1902.

In 1910 Roald Amundsen set sail in the *Fram*, intending to be the first explorer to reach the North Pole, only to discover en route that Robert Peary had beaten him to it. Not to be outdone, Amundsen turned the *Fram* around and, racing Robert Falcon Scott all the way, became the first man to reach the South Pole. Otto Sverdrup also sailed the schooner around southern Greenland to Canada's Nunavut region and Ellesmere Island between 1898 and 1902, travelling over 18,000km.

Ling Ling

no; Rådhusbrygge 4; mains 175-250kr, shrimp per kg 130kr; ⊗7am-11pm; 🚃Aker brygge)

Ling Ling

CANTONESE €€

12 🗶 Map p56, E3

Aker Brygge's culinary reputation has had a boost with the opening of this contemporary Asian restaurant and bar. Drawing inspiration from the Japanese *izakaya* food-pub concept, but serving Cantonese sharing plates, the dishes here are meant to be convivial and encourage sampling from the cocktail menu or beer or wine list. (☎24 13 38 00; http://lingling.hakkasan.com; Stranden 30; mains 155-385kr; ⊗5-10pm Sun-Thu, to 11pm Fri & Sat; 🚃Aker brygge)

Tjuvholmen Sjømagasin

SEAFOOD €€€

13 🗶 Map p56, D3

Fresh fish and seafood are beautifully prepared at this sleek, upmarket seafood place, with both traditional Norwegian (yes, it has fish soup) and international dishes (say, deep-sea turbot with fennel and burnt butter). There's also a shellfish bar where you can choose tank lobster or crab by the kilo, oysters or shrimp, or opt for a platter of them all (795kr per person). (☎23 89 77 77; www.sjomagasinet. no; Tjuvholmen allé 14; mains 295-385kr; ⊗11.30am-midnight Mon-Fri, from 1pm Sat; 🚃Aker brygge)

Understand
21st-Century Boomtown

Ten years ago, Oslo was a low-slung city, dominated only by the spires of its neoclassical churches. Today it's cranes that fill the skyline, testament to a building boom that not just rivals but has overtaken that of the late 19th century. Oslo is, in fact, Europe's fastest-growing capital. While the commercial and residential development of Bjørvika continues, along with many private developments scattered throughout the city and its neighbourhoods, there are a number of projects that will transform the city in the next decade.

Norway's new Nasjonalmuseet (National Museum) – housing collections from the once separate National Gallery, National Museum of Contemporary Art, and Museum of Decorative Arts and Design under one roof, in a design that emphasises 'dignity and longevity' – is scheduled for completion in 2020 and will be joined by Lambda, the new Munch Museet, shortly after that. This will be followed by an ambitious reimagining of the Regjeringskvartalet, the government quarter, to address both damage wrought by Anders Breivik's 2011 attack as well as creating a more pedestrian-friendly, dense urban core.

Still, the recent tumbling of oil prices (and the government's first hack into the nation's sovereign wealth fund) could well put the brakes on what has been halcyon days for property developers, city planners and young, ambitious architecture firms.

Some citizens are not unhappy about this, citing both Akker Brygge and Bjørvika's scattershot development, lack of social diversity and insensitivity to the Oslofjord environment as things that may have been avoided with a little restraint. But in typically thoughtful Norwegian style, there continues to be much work – from government, community groups, urban theorists and young entrepreneurs – devoted to ensuring the city remains a green, inclusive, prosperous and lively place well into the future.

Delicatessen TAPAS €€

14 🍴 Map p56, E2

This Grünerløkka favourite brings some welcome east-side cool to an industrial space in Akker Brygge, not to mention some of the city's best tapas. The large tapas menu takes in small dishes like saffron and chorizo croquettes and meatballs, plates of well-sourced Spanish *jamon* (ham) and artisan *manchego* (Spanish cheese), and larger plates of grilled octopus or chicken. (http://delicatessen. no; Holmens gate 2; tapas 68-149kr; ⏱11am-midnight Sun-Wed, to 1am Thu-Sat; 🚋Aker brygge)

Albert Bistro FRENCH €€€

15 🍴 Map p56, E2

Francophiles rejoice: you can get your French fix, from early-morning *croque monsieurs* and omelettes to a wide range of well-prepared bistro classics such as *carré d'agneau* (lamb cutlet), *moule frite* (mussels and chips) and *entrecôte* (steak). The space is no-surprises contemporary bistro-by-numbers but delightfully stylish and bright at that. (📞21 02 36 30; www. albertbistro.no; Stranden 3; mains 185-355kr; ⏱7.30am-11pm Mon-Fri, 9am-11pm Sat & Sun; 🚋Aker brygge)

Polarship Fram Museum (p58)

Bølgen & Moi SEAFOOD €€€

16 🍴 Map p56, D3

National chain Bølgen & Moi occupies a prime position overlooking the docks and is a good place for a summer-evening burger, pasta or fish soup and a drink. (📞22 44 10 20; www. bolgenogmoi.no; Tjuvholmen allé 5; mains 189-285kr; ⏱11am-10pm Mon-Sat, 3-9pm Sun; 🚋Aker brygge)

Explore

Frogner
& Western Oslo

The ever-affluent west side of Oslo – home to the most expensive
real estate in the country – may be largely residential, but its expans-
es of leafy streets of grand 19th-century apartment buildings and
villas fanning out from behind the Royal Palace and out to Frognerparken are a delight indeed. The area is also home to a few must-see
sights and a number of new, interesting eating and drinking places.

MORTEN FALCH SORTLAND/GETTY IMAGES ©

The Sights in a Day

☀ Jump on the T-bane or tram to get to **Vigelandsanlegget** (p66), a sculptural installation where you could well be overwhelmed by so much humanity. Loll on the grass at the pretty, bucolic **Frognerparken** (p70) to recover.

☼ Head to the **Vigeland Museum** (p70), also in the park, to see the sculptor's working methods and his original studio home, then picnic beneath the trees before heading off to find the charming **Oslo City Museum** (p74) just outside the southern entrance to the park.

☾ Wander back to the city down Frogner's well-to-do and architecturally satisfying streets, taking in the **Nasjonalbiblioteket** (p74) and the **Nobel Institute** (p74). Pop into **Oslo Contemporary** (p74) for interesting conceptual shows held in a former garage, then head to **Fyr Bistronomi** (p77) for dinner.

For a local's day in Frognerparken, see p70

◉ Top Sights
Vigelandsanlegget (p66)

◯ Local Life
Strolling Frogner (p70)

♥ Best of Oslo
Drinking
Champagneria (p78)

Shopping
Utopia Retro Modern (p78)

Nomaden (p78)

For Kids
Frognerparken (p70)

Free
Vigelandsanlegget (p66)

Getting There

🚋 **Tram** 12 and 13 run from the city and Grünerløkka.

🚆 **Train** Line 2 runs from Central to Majorstuen.

Top Sights
Vigelandsanlegget

Gustav Vigeland is Norway's best-loved sculptor and this collection of his work fills, and utterly transforms, the city's Frognerparken, with more than 200 sculptures in granite, bronze and iron. Vigeland by name, Vigeland by nature, this is the world's largest sculpture park dedicated to one artist; his hectares of figurative work are all in service to a circle-of-life theme.

Vigeland Sculpture Park

👁 Map p72, B3

www.vigeland.museum.no/no/vigelandsparken

Nobels gate 32

🕑 Tue-Sun noon-4pm

T Borgen

The Gate

The park's main entrance on Kirkeveien is marked with a grand granite and wrought-iron gate, or series of gates to be more precise, with curving railings on each side that meet copper-topped gatehouses. Despite their lovely organic geometry, they have an otherworldiness – perhaps in gentle preparation for the experience awaiting you within.

The Bridge

The 100m-long bridge was the first part of the park to be open and its sculptures of babies and children are its most enduring and endearing feature. It's here that you will find the much-documented *Sinnataggen*, the little Angry Boy, a bronze of a child in the full throes of a tantrum. Look up and you'll also notice unusual, rather jarring, science-fiction-like columns depicting humans in combat with large lizards.

The Fountain

Vigeland had long dreamed of a monumental fountain and its turn-of-the-century origins and Jugendstil influence are clear, although it was not until 1924 that this extraordinary work found its home. Its stylistic formality is highlighted by its bronze material and there's a rhythmic grace to the composition and siting. Twenty groups of trees shelter groups of human figures, depicting the journey from cradle to grave. The bronze reliefs which clad the outer side of the pool were not completed until 1947, after many changes. They too depict the eternal life cycle.

The Monolith

Flanked by steps lined with highly sensual couples in granite, the *Monolith* sits at the highest point of the park. Carved from a single enormous granite block, the tower rises more than 14m

JTB PHOTO/UIG VIA GETTY IMAGES ©

☑ Top Tips

▶ Visit Vigeland Museum (p70), Gustav Vigeland's former studio.

▶ For more Vigeland, head to the museum of Gustav's brother, the **Emanuel Vigeland Museum** (☎ 22 14 57 88; www.emanuelvigeland. museum.no; Grimelundsveien 8; adult/child 50kr/ free; ⊙ noon-5pm Sun May-Sep, to 4pm Oct-Apr; Ⓣ Smestad), a short trip further west.

✗ Take a Break

For drinks and snacks, Kafe Vigeland is right next to the main gate. If you're in need of a drink after all that nudity, Herregårdskroen, just before the Vigeland Museum, is a good option.

Wheel of Life by Gustav Vigeland

above its 3m plinth. The figures here clamber and climb over each other at the same time as holding each other and willing themselves ever upwards. After the emotionality of the bridge and the melancholy resignation of the fountain, it's a dynamic work of yearning and transcendence (if still an onslaught and not just a little bit creepy).

The Wheel of Life

Furthest from the park's entrance is the *Wheel of Life*, first modelled in 1933–34. Its simple form of entwined human figures speaks to the entire theme of the park, that of never-ending momentum where we both push eternally forward and cling to each other in support.

Other Sculptures

It's also worth seeking out the group of figures known as the Clan. With its 21 entwined figures, it's the largest work besides the Monolith. Just inside the main entrance, back by the gate, you can see Vigeland himself, a (self) portrait of the artist from 1942, tools to the ready and sporting his rustic sculpting uniform.

Vigelandsanlegget

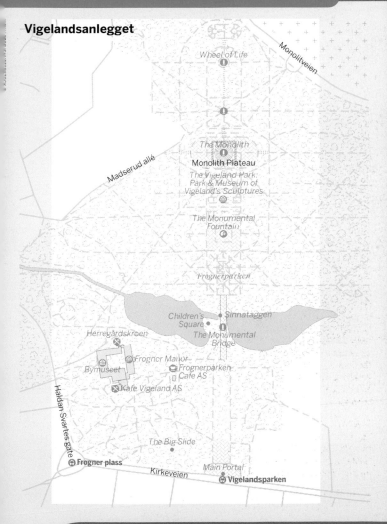

Monolitveien

Wheel of Life

The Monolith
Monolith Plateau

The Vigeland Park:
Park & Museum of
Vigeland's Sculptures

Madserud allé

The Monumental
Fountain

Frognerparken

Children's
Square   Sinnataggen

Herregårdskroen   The Monumental
Bridge

Frogner Manor
Bymuseet   Frognerparken
Cafe AS
Kafe Vigeland AS

Haldan Svartes gate

The Big Slide

Frogner plass   Main Portal
Kirkeveien   **Vigelandsparken**

Local Life
Strolling Frogner

West of the city, Frognerparken is one of Norway's most-visited attractions. Its centrepiece Vigelandsanlegget (p66) attracts huge numbers but many overlook the park itself, as well as the surrounding neighbourhood, which happens to be one of Oslo's prettiest and most well-to-do. Join locals for a laze in the grass on sunny days or a window shop or bite to eat.

❶ Get to Know Gustav

Gustav Vigeland's process – his plasters and preparatory drawings – are fascinating. See them at the **Vigeland Museum** (www.vigeland.museum.no; Nobelsgata 32; adult/child 60/30kr, with Oslo Pass free; ⏱10am-5pm Tue-Sun May-Aug, noon-4pm Tue-Sun rest of year; 🚌20, 🚌12, 🚌N12, Ⓣ Borgen), which is his former home and studio, before you come face-to-face with the famous works themselves; it makes the visit all the

more interesting. If you're visiting in the summer, join locals for afternoon classical-music concerts, with tickets sold on the day and including museum entrance.

2 Sculpture upon Sculpture

The sheer number of sculptures scattered throughout the park can almost overwhelm, and while all eyes are drawn to the *Monolith,* don't miss the *Wheel of Life* to its west, a tight coil of human figures expressing yet again Vigeland's persistent articulation of the cycle of life.

3 Take a Dip

It's well worth bringing your bathers and factoring in time for a dip if the weather is hot (yes, Oslo does get hot in high summer). Jo Nesbø fans will recognise the **Frognerbadet** (🏊23 27 54 50; Middelthuns gate 28; adult/child 98/48kr; ⏲7am-7.30pm Mon-Thu, to 8pm Fri-Sun Jun–mid-Aug; Ⓣ Borgen) pool only too well; it's the scene of one of the particularly nasty murders from his controversially grisly *The Leopard.*

4 Kiosk Stop

Stroll past the park's dark lake to Herregårdskroen, a pretty pale-yellow summer kiosk, a delightfully old-fashioned place. Have refreshments on its terrace and listen to the birdsong and rustling of the trees – beyond the main Vigeland axis the park returns to its serene self.

5 Bygdøy Allé

This neighbourhood has the most expensive real estate in the country. The blocks of magnificent 19th-century apartments along this strip are also some of Oslo's most decorative, and are where locals come to browse the interiors shops.

6 Pizza Paradise

After an afternoon in the outdoors, what better way to refuel but with pizza? **Villa Paradiso** (🏊917 67 639; www.villaparadisofrogner.com; Sommerrogata 17; mains 239-310kr, pizza 105-195kr; ⏲11am-11pm Mon-Fri, from noon Sat & Sun; 🚌30, 31, N12, N30, 🚋Solli) is a delightfully airy, tiled space that's always packed with pizza-obsessed westsiders, and is both fun and relaxed.

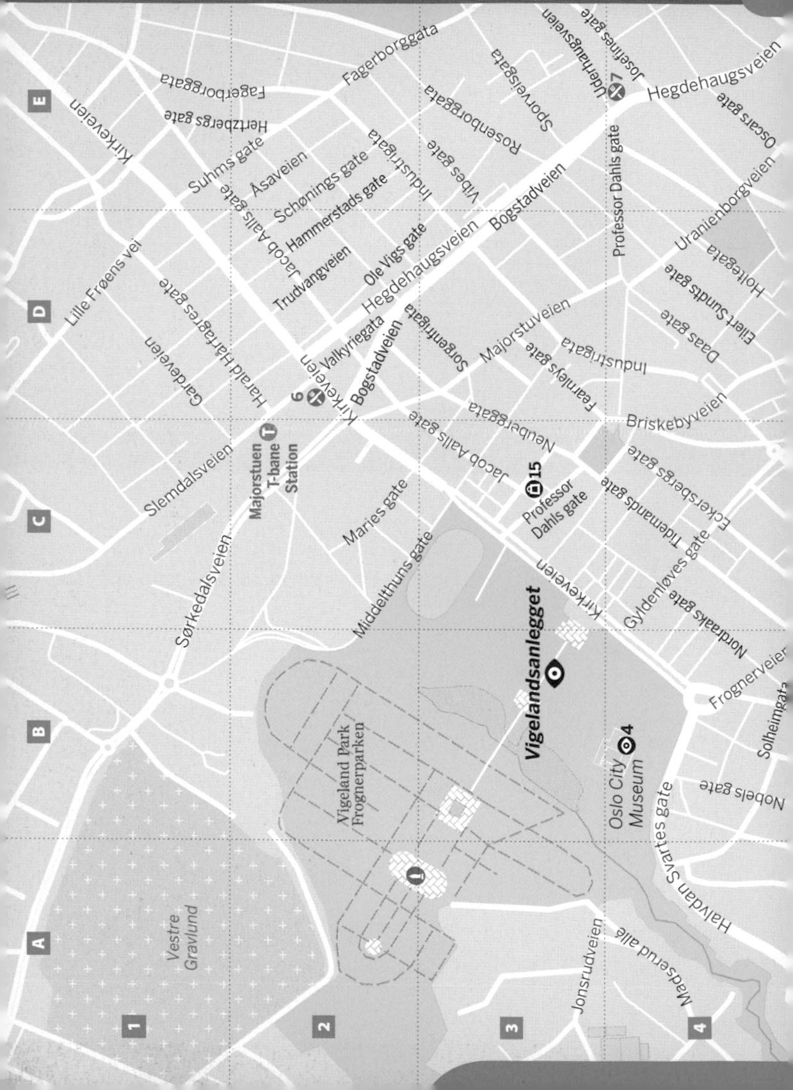

Kirkeveien

Lille Froens vei

Gardeveien

Slemdalsveien

Sørkedalsveien

Suhms gate

Asaveien

Jacob Aalls gate

Harald Hårfagres gate

Schønings gate

Hammerstads gate

Trudvangveien

Fagerborggata

Hertzbergs gate

Fagerborggata

Rosenborggata

Sporveisgata

Industrigata

Vibes gate

Sørensgata

Uddehaugsveien

Josefines gate

Hegdehaugsveien

Oscars gate

Professor Dahls gate

Uranienborgveien

Holtegata

Eilert Sundts gate

Daas gate

Industrigata

Ole Vigs gate

Hegdehaugsveien

Bogstadveien

Valkyriegata

Bogstadveien

Sørensgata

Majorstuveien

Fearnleys gate

Neubergata

Briskebyveien

Eckersbergs gate

Tidemands gate

6 ❌

Kirkeveien

Majorstuen
T-bane 🅣
Station

Jacob Aalls gate

Maries gate

🔘15

Professor
Dahls gate

Gyldenløves gate

Nordraaks gate

Frognerveien

Middelthuns gate

Kirkeveien

Vigelandsanlegget

🔘

Solheimgata

Nobels gate

Halvdan Svartes gate

Vestre
Gravlund

Nigeland Park
Frognerparken

Oslo City
Museum 🔘4

Madserud allé

Jonsrudveien

❶

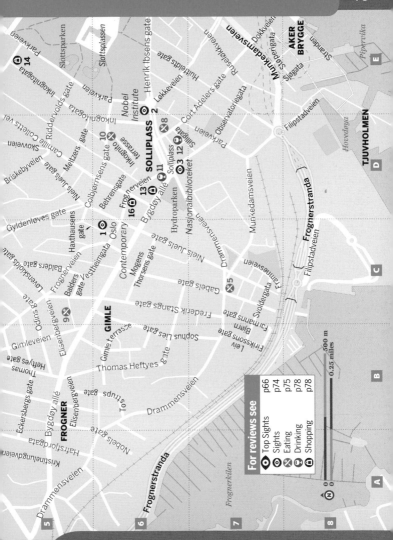

AKER BRYGGE

TJUVHOLMEN

SOLLIPLASS

GIMLE

FROGNER

Slottsparken

Slottsplassen

Parkveien

Henrik Ibsens gate

Nobel Institute

Inkognitogata

Inkognito terrasse

Behrensgate

Colbjørnsens gate

Niels Juels gate

Meltzers gate

Skovveien

Briskebyveien

Camilla Colletts vei

Riddervolds gate

Gyldenløves gate

Haxthausens gate

Frognerveien

Løvenskiolds gate

Balders gate

Odins gate

Elisenbergveien

Gimleveien

Thomas Heftyes gate

Gimle terrasse

Thomas Heftyes gate

Eckersbergs gate

Bygdøy allé

Elisenbergveien

Nobels gate

Hafrsfjordgata

Kristinelundveien

Drammensveien

Frognerstranda

Drammensveien

Sophus Lies gate

Frederik Stangs gate

Gabels gate

Thorsens gate

Mogens

Niels Juels gate

Contemporary Oslo

Bygdøy allé

Frognerveien

Drammensveien

Hydroparken

Nasjonalbiblioteket

Munkedamsveien

Fritznersgate

Svoldergata

Bjørn Farmanns gate

Leiv Eirikssons gate

Frognerstranda

Frognerveien

Filipstadveien

Cort Adelers gate

Observatoriegata

Parkveien

Sillgata

Ruseløkkveien

Huitfeldts gate

Løkkeveien

Munkedamsveien

Dokkveien

Stranden

Sjøgata

Støperigata

Filipstadveien

Frognerstranda

Pipervika

Hovedøya

Frognerkilen

1 Oslo

2

3

5

8

9

10

11

12

13

14

16

For reviews see

◉	Top Sights	p66
⊙	Sights	p74
✕	Eating	p75
🍸	Drinking	p78
🛍	Shopping	p78

500 m
0.25 miles

Sights

Oslo Contemporary
GALLERY

1 Map p72, C6

The westside's best commercial gallery. Set in a former garage, it represents an interesting line-up of emerging and established conceptual artists, mostly from Norway. (📞23 27 06 76; www.oslcontemporary.com; Haxthausens gate 3; ⏱noon-5pm Tue-Fri, to 4pm Sat; 🚋Niels Juels gate)

Nobel Institute
NOTABLE BUILDING, LIBRARY

2 Map p72, E6

It is unclear why Alfred Nobel chose Norway to administer the Peace Prize, but whatever the reason, it is a committee of five Norwegians, appointed for six-year terms by the Norwegian Storting (parliament), that chooses the winner each year, and their meetings are held here behind closed doors. You can, however, visit the library, which contains some 200,000 volumes on international history and politics, peace studies and economics. (📞22 12 93 00; www.nobelpeaceprize.org; Henrik Ibsens gate 51; admission free; ⏱8am-3pm Mon-Fri; 🚋Solli)

Nasjonalbiblioteket
LIBRARY

3 Map p72, D6

A thoroughly modern library where you can view important documents of Norway's cultural heritage, from 13th-century manuscripts to magazines, films and Norwegian musical scores. There are also temporary exhibitions highlighting various aspects of the collection. (National Library; 📞23 27 60 11; www.nb.no; Henrik Ibsens gate 110; admission free; ⏱9am-6pm Jun-Sep, 8.30am-3.30pm Mon-Fri Oct-May; 🚋Solli)

Oslo City Museum
MUSEUM

4 Map p72, B4

Near the southern entrance to Vigeland Park, this charming museum is housed in the 18th-century Frogner Manor, built on the site of a Viking-era great house. It's a lovely snapshot of traditional bourgeois Norwegian life of the era and there are other exhibitions about Oslo's urban history. (Oslo Bymuseet; 📞23 28 41 70; www.oslomuseum.no; Frognerveien 67; admission free; ⏱11am-4pm Tue-Sun; 🚋Solli)

☑ Top Tip

Skating & Swimming

Come winter, head to **Frogner Ice Skating Rink** (Map p72, 2C; 📞910 05 955; www.frognerstadion.no; Middelthunsgate 26; adult/child 40/15kr; ⏱11am-10pm Mon-Thu, to 9pm Fri, to 6pm Sat & Sun Dec-Mar; 🚇Borgen) for no-frills family fun. Skate hire is 100kr to 150kr per session.

In summer, Oslo's large and beautifully sited public pool Frognerbadet (p71) is a great place to cool off.

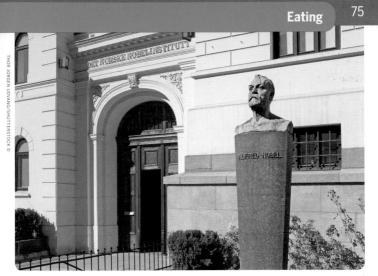

Nobel Institute

Eating

Hos Thea

NORWEGIAN €€€

5 Map p72, C7

Hos Thea manages to be both a reminder of that first bloom of gastronomic cooking in the capital (it's been going strong since 1987) and a friendly, warm locals' favourite for special-occasion nights out. Set in a former butcher's shop, it serves flavourful dishes that have the odd French flourish (think brioche and foie gras) or Italian base (risotto and ravioli) but remain quintessentially Norwegian. (✆22 44 68 74; www.hosthea. no; Gabelsgata 11; mains 340kr, 4-/6-course menu 555/755kr; ◷5-10pm Sun-Thu, to 10.30pm Fri & Sat; ☒Skillebekk)

Park 29

INTERNATIONAL €€€

6 Map p72, D2

Set in one of Oslo's oldest remaining wooden villas (once the home of composer Halfdan Kjerulf and later a legendary car dealer) and with a summer dining lawn, this must be one of Oslo's prettiest restaurants. A menu of simply if carefully done international and Norwegian classics is attractively plated and the upmarket wine list is a treat to sample. (✆481 70 000; www.park29.no; Parkveien 29; mains 295-335kr; ☒Riddervolds plass)

EDUCATION IMAGES/UIG VIA GETTY IMAGES ©

Self-portrait of Gustav Vigeland

Understand
Gustav Vigeland

The sculptor Gustav Vigeland (1869–1943) was born to a farming family near Mandal, in the far south of Norway. As a child and teenager he became deeply interested in Protestant spirituality, woodcarving and drawing – a unique combination that would dominate his life's work. In 1888 Vigeland secured an apprenticeship to sculptor Brynjulf Bergslien. The following year he exhibited his first work at the State Exhibition of Art. It was the break he needed, bringing his talents to national and international attention.

In 1891 Vigeland travelled to Copenhagen and then to Paris and Italy, where he worked with various masters; he was especially inspired by the work of French sculptor Auguste Rodin. When his public grants ran out he returned to Norway to make a living working on the restoration of the Nidaros Cathedral in Trondheim and producing commissioned portraits of prominent Norwegians.

In 1921, after decades of dedicated practice, his talents were recognised by the City of Oslo and a spacious studio was built for him; it's now a museum.

Fyr Bistronomi
NEW NORDIC €€

7 🍴 Map p72, E4

Westside well-to-do your fellow diners may be, but this is a delightfully casual place with a focus on grilled meats, from lobster and prawns to wagyu and pork neck. That said, it's definitely not a BBQ joint, with a light and artful hand with accompaniments, saucing, sides and snacks. The wine list is elegant, as are the cocktails. (www.fyrbistronomi.no; Underhaugsveien 28; mains 140-240kr; set menus 550-695kr; ⏰6-11pm Tue-Sat, lounge from 11.30am; 🚋Vigelandsparken)

Alex Sushi
SUSHI €€€

8 🍴 Map p72, D6

Sit around the elegant oval bar for what's widely considered Oslo's best sushi. You can order à la carte, but most regulars go the *omakase* route (the chef's selection; 1150kr); whichever you decide, expect perfection if not innovation. Dishes feature the very best of Norwegian seafood prepared simply alongside signature dishes such as the tempura salad and au gratin lobster. (📞22 43 99 99; www.alexsushi.no; Cort Adelers gate 2; set menus 495-1150kr; ⏰4-11pm; 🚋Solli)

Feinschmecker
NORWEGIAN €€€

9 🍴 Map p72, C5

While no longer bearing a Michelin star, this gastronomic place is a firm neighbourhood favourite with a menu of modern Norwegian dishes using excellent local produce. Despite its venerable status, you're more than welcome to drop in for a glass of wine and there's no pressure to make the set menu commitment. (📞22 12 93 80; www.feinschmecker.no; Balchens gate; mains 325-425kr, 4-/7-course menus 895/1395kr; ⏰5-9pm Mon-Sat; 🚋Elisenberg)

Åpent Bakeri
CAFE €

10 🍴 Map p72, D6

A neighbourhood cafe that serves coffee in deep, cream-coloured bowls and has unbeatable breads and pastries. A freshly baked roll topped with homemade *røre syltetøy* (stirred jam) and enjoyed on the bakery's patio makes for one of Oslo's most atmospheric breakfasts. (📞22 04 96 67; Inkognito terrasse 1; snacks 45-129kr; ⏰7.30am-5pm Mon-Fri, 9am-4pm Sat & Sun; 🚋Inkognitogata)

🔍 Local Life
Westside Eating

Westsiders now don't have to cross the city for their favourite eastside eating options or casual cool, with the increasingly buzzy Solliplass lined with good eating and drinking options, including the westside outpost of perenial Grünerløkka favourite, **Villa Paradiso** (Map p73, D6; 📞917 67 639; www.villaparadiso frogner.com; Sommerrogata 17; mains 239-310kr, pizza 105-195kr; ⏰11am-11pm Mon-Fri, from noon Sat & Sun; 🚌30, 31, N12, N30, 🚋Solli).

Q Local Life

Norwegian Wood Festival

Oslo plays host to dozens of music festivals but **Norwegian Wood** (Map p72, 2C; www.norwegian wood.no; ⏱Jun), held in the whimsical surrounds of the Frognerbadet (p71), is one of the most highly regarded. Its spot-on selection of Norwegian acts as well as international headliners draws a dedicated local crowd.

Drinking

Champagneria   WINE BAR

11 Map p72, D6

Yes, it has Champagne – a very detailed and long list, in fact – but also Spanish cava and Italian prosecco. Spread over two floors, this is a busy after-work option, with a short tapas selection of tummy-liners too. (☎21 08 09 09; www.champagneria.com; Frognerveien 2; ⏱4pm-1am Mon-Wed, to 3am Thu & Fri, 1pm-3am Sat, 4-11pm Sun; 🚋Solli)

Palace Bar   BAR

12 Map p72, D6

The place where the well-heeled crowd of Oslo West can be found sipping cocktails or downing beers. Its over-the-top back bar is covered with black and silver graffiti, with snakes, dolls and old phones preserved in bottles lining the shelves. The seven-table restaurant at the front does a 10-course daily menu, if you feel like making an evening of it. (Solligata 2; ⏱6-10pm Mon-Sat; 🚋Solli)

Shopping

Utopia Retro Modern   VINTAGE, HOMEWARES

13 🔒 Map p72, D6

Take note of this lovely 1929 functionalist shopfront before browsing the great mid-century design within; designed by Arne Korsmo and Sverre Aasland, it remains super-characteristic of the era. While you'll also find plenty of fantastic international pieces here, look out for the beautiful Norwegian design pieces, both original and reissued, from names like Torbjørn Afdal, Gunnar Sørlie and Sven Ivar Dysthe. (☎408 60 460; www.utopiaretromodern.com; Bygdøy allé 7; ⏱12.30-6pm Thu & Fri, 1-4pm Sat; 🚋Solli)

Nomaden   BOOKS

14 🔒 Map p72, E5

This is a classic travel bookshop where the shelves are bursting with guides, maps and travel literature that will have you dreaming of your next holiday in no time. (☎23 13 14 15; www.nomaden.no; Uranienborgveien 4; ⏱10am-6pm Mon-Fri, to 5pm Sat; 🚌17B)

JULIE MAYFENG/SHUTTERSTOCK ©

Vestkanttorget Flea Market

Vestkanttorget Flea Market
MARKET

15 🔒 Map p72, C3

If you're happy sifting through heaps of, well, junk in search of an elusive vintage band T-shirt or mid-century ceramic coffee pot, take a chance here. It's at the plaza that intersects Professor Dahls gate, a block east of Vigeland Park, and it's a more than pleasant way to pass a Saturday morning.

(Amaldus Nilsens plass; ⊘10am-4pm Sat; T Majorstuen)

Hassan og Den Dama
FASHION & ACCESSORIES

16 🔒 Map p72, D6

A Skovveien stalwart, this shop has clothing, shoes and jewellery produced by Scandinavian and international designers. (http://dendama.com; Skovveien 4; ⊘10am-6pm Mon-Fri, to 2pm Sat; 🚌 Solli)

Top Sights
Holmenkollen Ski Jump

Getting There

🚃 1 to Holmenkollen.

This beloved and historic Oslo landmark, perched on a hilltop overlooking the city, offers a classically Norwegian combination of adventure sport and great design (and, yes, fresh air and views). Home to March's annual Holmenkollen Ski Festival for over a century, it's one of the world's most visited sports facilities.

New Century Ski Jump

The various iterations of ski jump and stadium have been rebuilt 19 times during Holmenkollen's history, although we suspect the latest one will be around for a while. Designed by Danish-Belgian firm JDS Architects, it was officially opened with a 106.5m jump by champion Anette Sagen in March 2010. The design beautifully combines all the functions and uses of the site into one dramatic, dynamic form, a simplicity that draws all focus to the skiers, as well as serving as wind protection for the athletes themselves. A mesh of stainless steel clads the mesmerising swoop, rising 58m in the air; its 69m cantilever makes it the longest of its kind in the world.

A Century of Skiing

Long before there was a jump at Holmenkollen, people were propelling themselves down its scenic slope. Since 1892 it's been the site of the **Holmenkollen Ski Festival** (☎22 92 32 00; http://skifest.no/; Kongeveien 5; ☉early Mar) each March, a multiday event now so beloved by locals that 'Holmenkollen Sunday' is often jokingly referred to as Norway's second national day. A century ago skiers were pioneering jumps of 20m, but today's skiers regularly reach 140m or more.

The Oldest Skiing Museum in the World

The world's oldest **skiing museum** (Kongeveien 5; incl Holmenkollen Ski Jump adult/child 130/65kr, with Oslo Pass free; ☉9am-8pm Jun-Aug, 10am-5pm May & Sep, 10am-4pm rest of year; Ⓣ Holmen) – it opened in 1923 – takes in thousands of years of the art of carving up a mountain or gliding through the forest, including rock carvings of Stone Age off-piste and a pair of Viking skis, as well as a large exhibition dedicated to polar exploration and a fascinating look at snowboarding and the modern sport, climate and the Northern Lights. It's atmospherically set into the mountain with the ski jump towering above.

CCELIAPHOTO/GETTY IMAGES ©

☎916 71 947

www.holmenkollen.com

adult/child 130/65kr, with Oslo Pass free

☉9am-8pm Jun-Aug, 10am-5pm May & Sep, 10am-4pm rest of year

☑ Top Tips

▶ Holmenkollen can be reached by public transport in 20 minutes.

▶ Pack a picnic and make a day of it with a hike in nearby Nordmarka.

✕ Take a Break

The **Lysebu Hotel** (☎21 51 10 00; www.lysebu.no; Lysebuveien 12; s/d 1900/2300kr; Ⓟ🛜🐾; Ⓣ Voksenkollen), a quick metro trip away or a 50-minute walk, has a beautiful upmarket Neo Nordic dining room. Hike up to Nordmarka and grab a waffle at **Ullevålseter** (www.ullevalseter.no; Maridalen; waffles 35-59kr; ☉10am-4pm Tue-Fri, 9am-7pm Sat & Sun).

Explore

Grünerløkka & Vulkan

One glance at Grünerløkka – 'Løkka' will do fine – and you'll wonder if it's possible to pack in another bar, cafe, vintage shop or live-music venue. Join Oslo's flourishing creative classes (including students from the nearby art and design schools) for coffee-sipping, small-plate-picking, wine-quaffing and beer-swilling. And the action continues across the Akerselva in the revitalised warehouse district of Vulkan.

The Sights in a Day

☼ Start where it all began at **Olaf Ryes plass**, surrounded by some of the neighbourhood's most enduring favourite bars, restaurants, cafes and music venues, then explore the surrounding streets after a morning coffee at legendary **Tim Wendelboe** (p94).

☼ Wander down to the **Akerselva River** (p87) for some intriguing industrial architecture and some surprisingly wild stretches of rapids and lushly treed banks. To the north you'll find two of the city's best commercial galleries, **Rod Bianco** (p85) and **Standard** (p87). Then head back to **Mathallen Oslo** (p89) for lunch.

☽ Drinks and dinner can be had at **Territoriet** (p94) and **Le Benjamin** (p91). More-restless grazers or bar-hoppers could strike out to Torgatta or Fredensborgveien, and those in search of live music, dancing or just a late, late night should head to Vulkan and the venues just up the hill in Møllergata.

For a local's day in Grünerløkka, see p85.

🔍 Local Life

Alternative Grünerløkka (p85)

🖤 Best of Oslo

Eating

Bass (p88)

Pjoltergeist (p88)

Syverkiosken (p89)

Munchies (p90)

Villa Paradiso (p90)

Wünderburger (p84)

Drinking

Territoriet (p94)

Torggata Botaniske (p94)

Bettola (p96)

Dr Kneipp's Vinbar (p90)

Grünerløkka Brygghus (p96)

Crowbar & Brewery (p95)

Mir (p94)

Paul's Boutique (p85)

Getting There

🚊 **Tram** 11, 12 and 13 run directly through Grünerløkka into the city.

🚌 **Bus** 21 runs from Grünerløkka's Sannergata west into St Hanshaugen and down to Akker Brygge.

Local Life
Alternative Grünerløkka

Come and live la vida Løkka with the city's young and bohemian set. This once solidly proletarian enclave, a sensible grid of 19th-century apartments built to house the workers from the factories that lined the nearby Akerselva, is today Oslo's epicentre of bar, restaurant and cafe life. The country's largest art and design school is also here (art students *always* know how to have fun) and there's a number of galleries too.

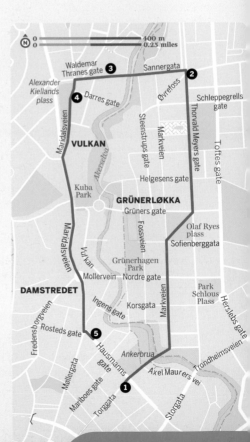

❶ Burger Time

Start your exploration with a build-your-own burger from **Wünderburger** (p90), an always-packed place on Torggata. The patties are all grass-fed beef from the west coast island of Lofoten and cooked to order. In summer grab a beer and head to a chair outside to watch the parade go by on this pedestrianised party zone.

❷ Supreme Roastworks

You'll pass at least one cafe on every corner as you wander up through Grünerløkka, but you'll find the locals with their laptops at **Supreme Roastworks** (📞22 71 42 02; www.srw. no; Thorvald Meyers gate 18a; ⏱7am-5pm; 🚃Birkelunden). Along with the legendary Tim Wendelboe, this is one of the neighbourhood's, and Oslo's, finest, run by an award-winning barista, and offers espresso-based coffees, drip or hand-filters (J60 or Chemex)...watch the beans being roasted while you drink.

❸ Art Market

Commercial and independent and art-run spaces dot the whole neighbourhood, but you'll have to walk a little further and look a little harder to find **Rod Bianco** (📞997 87 475; http://rodbian co.com; Waldemar Thranes gate 84c; ⏱noon-5pm Tue-Fri, to 4pm Sat; 🚃30). With a rota of envelope-pushing artists, including bad-boy art star Bjarne Melgaard, it's worth it. Head out the back and take the stairs just before the mechanic's

workshop. Check for openings and events too – all are welcome.

❹ Terrace Time or Ping-Pong?

The terrace tables at **Paul's Boutique** (📞483 87 730; www.facebook.com/Pauls BoutiqueOslo; Darres gate 1; ⏱2pm-12.30am Sun-Thu, to 3am Fri & Sat; 🚃54) are at a premium whenever the sun is out, for afternoon beers with a view of the grassy green triangle of Alexander Kiellands plass. Locals escape up here to avoid the weekend throng around Olaf Ryes plass, though their ping-pong comps and hip-hop nights are also a huge draw.

❺ Kafe Hærverk

Hausmanns gate totally goes off on weekend nights (and often during the week too), with a strip of venues lining both the street itself and those running down into Vulkan's riverside fun. **Kafe Hærverk** (📞930 95 357; www. kafe-haerverk.com; Hausmanns gate 34; ⏱6pm-3.30am Mon-Fri, from 4pm Sat & Sun; 🚃54) is hidden up some stairs in one of its solid old buildings and is known for its fascinating electronica acts, indie bands and very drinkable drinks, including natural wine.

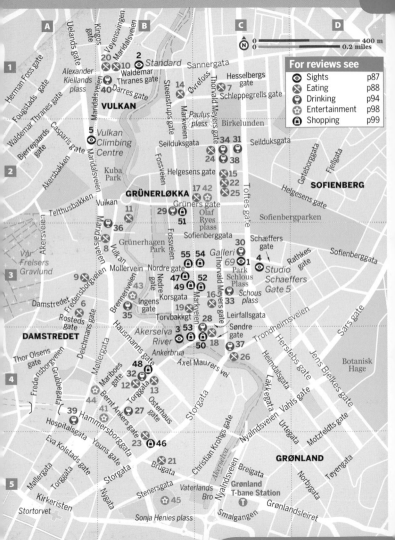

For reviews see

◉	Sights	p87
✖	Eating	p88
▤	Drinking	p94
✿	Entertainment	p98
🛍	Shopping	p99

MAREMAGNUM/GETTY IMAGES ©

Akerselva River

Sights

Galleri 69   GALLERY

1 ◉ Map p86, C3

Part of the Grünerløkka Lufthavn artists' studio and rehearsal space complex, this artist-run gallery has a monthly calendar of shows, with site-specific work produced exclusively for it. Check the website for opening hours. (☏22 38 00 28; http://lufthavna.no/galleri-69/; Toftes gate 69; ☐Schous plass)

Standard   GALLERY

2 ◉ Map p86, B1

A decade-plus player in Oslo's contemporary art scene, Standard has two exhibition spaces in an industrial block. It shows a range of Norwegian and northern European artists, including current Oslo darling Matias Faldbakken. (☏22 60 13 10; http://standardoslo.no; Waldemar Thranes gate 86; ◷noon-5pm Tue-Fri, to 4pm Sat; ☐30)

Akerselva River   RIVER

3 ◉ Map p86, B4

Running from Maridalsvannet to the Oslofjord, this fast-flowing river was once the centre of Oslo's industry and then, until the late 20th century, abandoned and unloved. Today it's one of the city's favourite places to relax, an 8km swath of forested rapids, waterfalls, running tracks, picnic grounds, swimming holes and fishing spots. The crashing falls at Beier Bridge are an inner-urban wonder. (🚇54)

Studio Schaeffers Gate 5

GALLERY

4 Map p86, C3

An independent artist-run space that hosts regular shows as well as events and performances. Check the website for details of seasonal shows. (📞452 18 078; www.schaeffersgate5.no; Schaeffers Gate 5; ⏲4-7pm Thu & Fri, from 1pm Sat & Sun; 🚋Schous plass)

Vulkan Climbing Centre

CLIMBING

5 Map p86, A2

Indoor climbing centre with challenges for all skill levels. The centre has climbing walls and bouldering walls. Open afternoons only during the week from June to August. (📞22 11 28 90; www.kolsaas.no; Maridalsveien 17; adult/child from 80/65kr; ⏲10am-10pm Mon-Thu, to 9pm Fri, to 8pm Sat & Sun; 🚇54)

Eating

Pjoltergeist

NEW NORDIC, KOREAN €€

6 Map p86, A3

One peek into this dim basement space and the intrigue begins, only to grow when you discover the menu. Icelandic chef Atly Mar Yngvason combines ingredients from his home country and his adopted Norwegian home, with the techniques and seasonings of Korea and Japan. Flavours are always bold, ingredients occasionally confronting (moose heart!), and the presentation insouciantly playful. (📞402 37 788; http://pjoltergeist.no; Rosteds gate 15; ⏲6pm-12.30am Tue-Sat; 🚇54)

Bass

NEW NORDIC €€

7 Map p86, C1

In what could be yet another Grünerløkka corner cafe, you'll find one of the city's best small-plate dining options, served beneath vintage seascapes on classic Norwegian ceramics by jovial Løkka locals. Most dishes are what might be called contemporary Norwegian-meets-international – from fried chicken and potato pancakes to deep-sea cod in sorrel butter and death-by-chocolate cake. (📞482 41 489; http://bassoslo.no; Thorvald Meyers gate 26; dishes 70-175kr; ⏲5pm-1am Tue-Sat, 3-8pm Sun; 🚋Birkelunden)

Kontrast

NEW NORDIC €€€

8 Map p86, B3

A minimalist, industrial space makes a dramatic backdrop for beautifully presented, seasonal dishes that combine a pure simplicity and honed technique. Peak season, organic and ethically sourced produce is used, including free-range or wild animals. Its recent Michelin star means you'll need to book well in advance. (📞21 60 01 01; www.restaurant-kontrast.no; Maridalsveien 15a; 6/10 courses 950/1250kr, small plates 135-225kr; ⏲6pm-midnight Tue-Sat; 🚇54)

Bon Lio
SPANISH, GASTRONOMIC €€€

9 Map p86, A3

You might expect some cultural dissonance between a Spanish gastronomic kitchen and a sweetly Norwegian wooden house, but it all comes together in a convivial and rather sexy manner. Bon Lio eschews formality but requires commitment: booking is mandatory, as is the tasting menu. Submit, and a multicourse feast of Mediterranean technique, Norwegian produce and occasional Asian flourishes will ensue. (☏467 77 212; http://bonlio.no; Fredensborgveien 42; menu 795kr; ⏲6pm-12.30am Tue-Fri, from 5pm Sat; ☐34)

Syverkiosken
HOT DOGS €

10 Map p86, B1

It might look like a hipster replica, but this hole-in-the-wall *pølser* (hot dogs) place is absolutely authentic and one of the last of its kind in Oslo. Dogs can be had in a potato bread wrap in lieu of the usual roll, or with both, and there's a large range of old-school accompaniments beyond bread sauce and mustard. (☏967 08 699; Maridalsveien 45; hot dogs from 20kr; ⏲9am-11.30pm Mon-Fri, from 11am Sat & Sun; ☐34)

Mathallen Oslo
FOOD HALL €€

11 Map p86, B2

Down by the river, this former industrial space is now a food court dedicated to showcasing the very best of Norwegian regional cuisine, as well as some excellent internationals. There are dozens of delis, cafes and miniature restaurants, and the place buzzes throughout the day and well into the evening. (www.mathallenoslo.no; Maridalsveien 17, Vulkan; ⏲8am-1am Tue-Fri, from 9.30am Sat & Sun; ☐54)

Taco República
TACOS €

12 Map p86, B4

After years of Tex-Mex mashups, Oslo has finally got a proper taqueria, a bright school-chair-strewn space, with a great range of tacos stuffed with fresh, locally sourced and homemade fillings (the various fish ones are particularly tasty). Note: all the tacos are made on the premises and are gluten-free. (☏400 57 665; http://tacorepublica.no; Torggata 30; tacos 58-70kr; ⏲noon-11pm

Local Life
Fairy-tale Crossing

There are plenty of places to cross the Akerselva, all of them picturesque. Yes, the views from the **Ankerbrua bridge** (Map p86, 4B) are pretty, but its Dyre Vaa's bronzes from 1937 lining each side that will linger in your memory. These depict scenarios from classic Norwegian folk tales by Asbjørnsen and Moe, including *Peer Gynt*, *Kari Trestakk* and the particularly striking *White-Bear-King-Valemon*, represented here by a depiction of a naked princess mounting a large and rather happy bear.

Tue-Thu, 12.30pm-12.30am Fri & Sat, 2-10pm Sun; 🚊34)

Wünderburger BURGERS €

13 🍴 Map p86, B4

You'll find excellent Oslo burgers here, using free-range Lofoten beef, brioche buns and build-your-own choices. The veggie burgers are also good, and the gluten-free buns better than the usual. (Torggata 37; burgers 90-120kr; ⏰11am-10pm Mon-Thu, to 3am Fri, noon-3am Sat, 1-11pm Sun; 🚊34)

Liebling CAFE €

14 🍴 Map p86, B1

One of the nearby KHiO (Oslo National Academy of the Arts) kids' cafes of choice, this 'Berlin-style' corner gem is a great place to kick back with your laptop and a late, late breakfast. There's a huge range of pastries and cakes, including raw and gluten-free options; coffee is care of Supreme Roastworks, and there's beer and German and Austrian wines. (☑24 02 23 02; Øvrefoss 4; plates 125kr, sandwiches 65-85kr; ⏰8am-8pm Tue-Fri, from 10am Sat-Mon; 🚊Birkelunden)

Munchies BURGERS €

15 🍴 Map p86, C3

Munchies might be perpetually crowded and those extras can add up, but its burgers and fries definitely put it in the city's best burger options. Grab a window stool and sample its craft beers too. (http://munchies.no; Thorvald Meyers gate 36; burgers 92-115kr; ⏰11am-

10pm Sun-Wed, to midnight Thu, to 3am Fri & Sat; 🚊Schous plass)

Kamai ASIAN €€

16 🍴 Map p86, C3

You get two restaurants here for the price of one: a shopfront casual canteen and takeaway doing sushi and *bao* (steam buns); and a restaurant hidden across the courtyard upstairs, serving elegant Nordic-Asian fusion small plates such as smoked reindeer heart, eel and potato, or salmon with wasabi and cabbage. (☑23 89 79 66; www.kamai. no; Korsgata 25; dishes 129-175kr, 4-course meal 485kr, bao and sushi 70-210kr; ⏰restaurant 5pm-1am Wed-Sun, takeaway 3-9pm Mon-Fri, 11am-11pm Sat; 🚊Schous plass)

Villa Paradiso PIZZA €€

17 🍴 Map p86, C2

Overlooking Grünerløkka's central park, with summertime al fresco dining next to an old Italian car, this place is rated by many as serving some of the best pizza in the capital – no minor feat in a city obsessed with pizza. Always full, always happy. (☑22 35 40 60; www.villaparadiso.no; Olaf Ryes plass 8; pizza 154-194kr; ⏰8am-11pm Mon-Fri, from 10am Sat & Sun; 🚊Olaf Ryes plass)

Dr Kneipp's Vinbar NORWEGIAN €€

The casual little sibling to Markveien Mat & Vinhus (see 19 Map p86, B3), Dr Kneipp's is the place for sipping wines by the glass (there are around 400 wines to choose from) accompanied

Tim Wendelboe (p94)

by light, snacky dishes such as cured mackerel or an Italian-style *carne crudo* (raw beef), or dishes from Markveien's menu. The baked cheesecake is legendary. (📞22 37 22 97; www.markveien.no; Torvbakkgt 12; mains 175-265kr; ⏰4pm-1am Mon-Sat; 🚊Schous plass)

Le Benjamin
FRENCH €€€

18 Map p86, C4

Mais oui, it's proper French bistro dining here, refined but relaxed, with classics such as fried sardines, poached pigeon, salt-baked turbot, beef marrow on toast and of course a *plat du jour*. There's a very good wine list heavy on French vintages too. Book ahead for a table or come early for an almost-Parisian terrace seat. (📞22 35 79 44; www.lebenjamin.no; Søndre gate 6; mains 248-310kr; ⏰4-11pm Tue-Sun; 🚊Schous plass)

Markveien Mat & Vinhus
NORWEGIAN €€€

19 Map p86, B3

For a cosy, traditional Norwegian dining room, this lovely spot on the southern edge of Grünerløkka is hard to better. Settle in at one of the candlelit tables and tuck into hearty, traditional (and sometimes international) dishes, such as lamb shank with root vegetables, confit duck leg with lentils or monkfish with radish and summer cabbage. (📞22 37 22 97;

MAREMAGNUM/GETTY IMAGES ©

Grünerløkka

www.markveien.no; Torvbakkgt 12; mains 280-325kr, 3/5 courses 455/615kr; ⏰4pm-1am Mon-Sat; 🚇Heimdalsgata)

Kasbah
MIDDLE EASTERN €

20 Map p86, B1

A basement hang-out specialising in filling falafels, filled pittas and mezze platters. It's as relaxing as throwing on a pair of Moroccan slippers, with sofas to lounge around on, reggae on the stereo and thrift-store decor to match. (📞21 94 90 99; www.thekasbah.no; Kingos gate 1b; mains 98-165kr, meze dishes 47-79kr; ⏰11am-1am Mon-Fri; 🚇Biermanns gate)

Teddy's Soft Bar
AMERICAN €

21 Map p86, B5

The jukebox in the corner gives Teddy's Soft Bar a flavour of 1950s USA. It's something of a local institution that has scarcely changed in decades. Its burgers go well with that other 1950s American favourite – milkshakes – though it's as much a place for a beer as a meal. (📞22 17 36 00; Brugata 3a; mains 95-120kr; ⏰11am-1am Mon-Sat; 🚇Brugata)

Hotel Havana
SPANISH €

22 Map p86, C2

With blue-and-white Andalucian tiles, this little place models itself on a Spanish bar. The food is likewise Spanish but with a Norwegian twist, such as a Bergen-style fish soup popping up for lunch. There's also a basic

tapas list for soaking up the jugs of sangria. (📞23 23 03 23; www.hotelhavana.no; Thorvald Meyers gate 38; mains 80-120kr; ⏰10am-midnight Sun-Wed, to 1am Thu, to 2am Fri & Sat; 🚇Brugata)

Far East
ASIAN €

23 Map p86, B5

Come for light and fresh Thai and Vietnamese curries, soups and noodles at this simple and very popular little place. (📞22 20 56 28; Bernt Ankers gate 4; mains 80-120kr; ⏰1pm-midnight; 🚇Brugata)

Nighthawk Diner
BURGERS €€

24 Map p86, C2

An all-American diner homage à la Edward Hopper, right down to the booth seats, jukebox, ketchup caddies and art-deco-style mirrored bar. Nighthawk serves burgers, shakes and hot dogs, and uses locally sourced beef and homemade sauces. (📞966 27 327; www.nighthawkdiner.com; Seilduksgata 15; mains 159-269kr; ⏰7am-11pm Mon-Thu, to 1am Fri, 10am-1am Sat, 10am-11pm Sun; 🚇Birkelunden)

Local Life
Park Life

On a sunny day there's no better place to be than **Grünerhagen** (Map p86, B3), the steep grassy slope at the end of Grünersgate. Join the locals and students for some tops-off R&R and wish you too had your own mini-grill for an impromptu BBQ.

Mucho Mas
MEXICAN €€

25 ✕ Map p86, C2

What it lacks in Mexican authenticity, Mucho Mas more than makes up for in cheese and portion size. The full Tex-Mex repertoire is on offer, including tacos, nachos and burritos (which are enormous); all dishes are offered in meat or vegetarian versions. Well-priced beer helps put out the fire. (☑22 37 16 09; www.muchomas.no; Thorvald Meyers gate 36; mains 95-210kr; ⊘noon-midnight Mon-Thu, to 3am Fri & Sat; 🚊Olaf Ryes plass)

Süd Øst
INTERNATIONAL €€€

26 ✕ Map p86, C4

With a large outdoor terrace overlooking the river for sunseekers, this upmarket place specialises in Southeast Asian fusion flavours. You can also just pop in for its Asian-influenced cocktails. (☑23 35 30 70; www.sudost.no; Trondheimsveien 5; mains 165-299kr; ⊘11am-11pm Sun-Thu, to 1am Fri & Sat; 🚊Heimdalsgata)

Drinking

Torggata Botaniske
COCKTAIL BAR

27 🍷 Map p86, B4

The greenhouse effect done right, with a lush assortment of indoor plants (including a warm herb-growing area) as well as beautiful mid-century light fittings and chairs, chandeliers, and lots of marble and mirrors. If you're not already seduced by the decor, the drinks will do it, with a list that features the bar's own produce, fresh fruit and good-quality spirits. (☑980 17 830; Torggata 17b; ⊘5pm-1am Sun-Wed, to 2am Thu, 2pm-3am Fri & Sat; 🚊Brugata)

Territoriet
WINE BAR

28 🍷 Map p86, C4

A true neighbourhood wine bar that's also the city's most exciting. The grape-loving owners offer up more than 300 wines by the glass and do so without a list. Talk to the staff about your preferences and – yes, this is Norway – your budget, and they'll find something you'll adore. Ordering beer or gin and tonic won't raise an eyebrow, we promise. (http://territoriet.no/; Markveien 58; ⊘4pm-1am Mon-Fri, from noon Sat & Sun; 🚊Schous plass)

Tim Wendelboe
CAFE

29 🍷 Map p86, B2

Tim Wendelboe is often credited with kick-starting the Scandinavian coffee revolution and his eponymous cafe and roastery is both a local freelancers' hang-out and an international coffee-fiend pilgrimage site. All the beans are, of course, self-sourced and hand-roasted (the roaster is part of the furniture), and all coffees – from an iced pour-over to a regular cappuccino – are world-class. (☑400 04 062; www.timwendelboe.no; Grüners gate 1; ⊘8.30am-6pm Mon-Fri, 11am-5pm Sat & Sun; 🚊Schous plass)

Mir
BAR

30 🍷 Map p86, C3

Part of the Grünerløkka Lufthavn complex – a collective cultural centre set

Mucho Mas

around a typical garden courtyard and home to many local artists, performers and musicians – Mir is pure Grünerløkka good times with space-station decor (they'll even lend you a space helmet), craft beers, house-blend chilli vodka, and daily entertainment such as electronic acts, improv jazz, DJs and quiz nights. (📞22 37 39 70; http://lufthavna.no; Toftes gate 69; ⏰6pm-1am; 🚃Schous plass)

Oslovelo

BAR

31 🚇 Map p86, C2

Celebrate cycling at this light and friendly cafe and bar. It does all-day breakfast with coffee from Supreme and serves all manner of beers, including those from the Grüner-

løkka Brewery, with DJs later in the evening. If you're travelling with your bike, it's also somewhere you can get repairs or buy parts. (📞23 23 05 53; www.oslovelo.com; Seilduksgata 23; ⏰10am-3.30am Mon-Fri, from 9am Sat, 10am-1am Sun; 🚃Birkelunden)

Crowbar & Brewery

BREWERY

32 🚇 Map p86, B4

Huge, rustic industrial brewery spread over two floors. They brew their own as well as pouring brews from Haandbryggeriet, Lindheim, Amundsen and Voss, along with some interesting Danish, Swedish and New World beers. (☑21 38 67 57; http://crowbryggeri. com/; Torggata 32; ⏲3pm-3am; 🚊34)

Hytta
BAR

33 Map p86, C3

So many Løkka bars, so little time. This one will grab your attention for its happy intimacy and towering bar stools, as well as Zeppelin on the turntable. For something that swings a little prog rock, the wine by the glass is rather good. (☑45 40 55 52; Thorvald Meyers gate 70; ⏲2pm-3am; 🚊Schous plass)

Bar Boca
BAR

34 Map p86, C2

A proper local's hang-out with an '80s-dive-bar vibe and super-welcoming staff. Beers go down well here, but they're also quite skilled with classic cocktails. It gets very busy at weekends and will be full when nowhere else is. A Grünerløkka must. (☑22 04 13 77; Thorvald Meyers gate 30; ⏲11am-1am Sun-Thu, to 3am Fri & Sat; 🚊Olaf Ryes plass)

Bortenfor
BAR

35 Map p86, B3

The only sign Bortenfor is there is the gate on Brenneriveien, so if you're lost best head for the bridge by stalwart club-bar Blå, but instead turn right and keep going. Along with the riverside beauty you'll get a cosy, cultured atmosphere, good music, Norwegian-themed cocktails and very decent wine by the glass. (☑922

66 683; http://ingensteds.no; Brenneriveien 7; ⏲4pm-1am Tue-Sun; 🚊54)

Hendrix Ibsen
COFFEE

36 Map p86, B3

Perfect place to grab a takeaway coffee for Akkerselva wandering, but you'll probably be tempted to linger over the racks of vintage vinyl or to pick up a bag of an interesting local roast coffee or hang out for an early-evening DJ performance. (☑457 97 150; http:// hendrixibsen.rocks; Vulkan 20; ⏲Mon-Thu 8am-11pm, to 3.30pm Fri & Sat, 10am-1pm Sun; 🚊54)

Bettola
COCKTAIL BAR

37 Map p86, C4

Mid-century furniture, a pretty tiled floor and friendly bar staff give this corner bar a welcoming vibe. It does one of the city's best negronis, and both the cocktail and wine lists are very well priced. (www.facebook.com/ bettolacocktailbar; Trondheimsveien 2; ⏲4pm-1am Mon-Thu, to 3am Fri & Sat)

Grünerløkka Brygghus
PUB

38 Map p86, C2

This atmospheric alehouse and micro-brewery does a range of house brews from pilsners to *Weißbiers*. Bottled beers include rarities such as sour *surøls* and Scandinavian Christmas beers. Stomach liners – burgers, bangers and mash, and fish and chips – can be ordered at the bar. Streetside benches are at a premium but worth

Understand
Live & Loud

Oslo has a thriving live-music scene – it's said that the city hosts more than 5000 gigs a year. Its venues are spread across the city but concentrate on Møllergata, in Vulkan, Grünerløkka and Grønland.

The year-round live calendar goes into overdrive in late spring, summer and early autumn with a rota of internationally respected music festivals. The largest of these, in fact the largest in Norway, is **Øya** (www.oyafestivalen.com; Tøyenparken; day passes 950kr; ☉early Aug; ⊤Tøyen), held in the eastside Tøyenparken. It's not only large but super green with its multiple stages powered through renewable energy and all rubbish recycled. **OverOslo** (www.overoslo.no; Grefsenkollveien 100; ☉Jun) makes the most of the city's stunning natural surrounds, its three-day festival held in a forested natural amphitheatre to the city's north with views all the way down to the Oslofjord. Closer to home again is Scandi-focused Norwegian Wood (p78), in the pretty surrounds of Frognerbadet.

What should be on your Oslo playlist? Here's a checklist of tunes across a variety of styles and eras to get you started.

Lindstrøm & Prins Thomas (Lindstrøm & Prins Thomas; 2005) Space disco with big drops and lots of highs from DJ master duo.

Dead Cats (Captain Credible; 2015) Epic crazy scientist solo electronica.

Scandinavian Leather (Turbonegro; 2003) Glammy proggy 'deathpunk' reunion album, the Oslo phenomenon's biggest seller.

Staying (Diskjokke; 2009) Minimal Scando-electronica from the great remixer.

Hunting High & Low (A-Ha; 1986) Go on, you know you want it.

Massive Cauldron of Chaos (1349; 2014) Blackest of black metal.

trying to snare. (www.brygghus.no; Thorvald Meyers gate 30; ☺3pm-1am Mon & Tue, to 2am Wed & Thu, to 3am Fri, noon-3am Sat, to midnight Sun; 🚊Olaf Ryes plass)

Villa

CLUB

39 🚇 Map p86, A4

With arguably the best sound system in the city, this is a diehard house-and electro-music club. In addition to Friday and Saturday, check for the occasional special Thursday gigs. (www.thevilla.no; Møllergata 23; ☺11pm-3am Fri & Sat; 🚊Brugata)

Colonel Mustard

PUB

40 🚇 Map p86, B1

Large vintage-furniture-filled pub named for a character from the board-game Cluedo. There's a large range of beers on tap, lots of cosy nooks to settle into and Cluedo to play. If you're hungry, the fish-and-chip, risotto or osso buco dinners are good bets. (📞21 95 05 00; http://colonelmustard.no; Darres gate 2; ☺11am-1am Sun-Thu, to 3am Fri & Sat; 🚊54)

Top Tip

DIY Drinks

If you're self-catering or considering DIY drinks before going out, in order to avoid Norway's high bar prices, note that while supermarkets sell beer, you can only buy wine and spirits from a Vinmonopolet (p101) shop. These are only open to around 6pm, and are closed on Sundays.

Entertainment

Rockefeller Music Hall   LIVE MUSIC

41 Map p86, B4

One of the city's best concert halls was once a bathhouse. It now hosts a wide range of artists and events. (www.rockefeller.no; Torggata 16; 🚊Brugata)

Parkteatret   LIVE MUSIC

42 ⭐ Map p86, C2

Oslo's beloved medium-sized venue, right on the lovely main square. Come to see international acts such as Shabazz Palaces or locals like Lindstrom and Anna of the North. (📞22 35 63 00; http://parkteatret.no; Olaf Ryes plass 11; 🚊Olaf Ryes plass)

Blå   LIVE MUSIC, DANCE

43 ⭐ Map p86, B3

Blå is all things to everyone, with DJs (it happens to be the city's best spot for hip-hop), live gigs and jazz. On Sundays there is a live big band that's been playing every afternoon for years. Or just come early for a drink at one of the pretty riverside tables. (www.blaaoslo.no; Brenneriveien 9c; ☺1pm-4am; 🚊54)

Revolver   LIVE MUSIC

44 ⭐ Map p86, A4

Dark and (slightly) dirty rock-and-roll bar with an attached band room. A great place to see a local or interesting international act or just to hang at the front bar with a musician-heavy

Blå

crowd. (☏22 20 22 32; www.revolveroslo.no; Møllergata 32; ☽6pm-3.30am; ▣Brugata)

Oslo Spektrum

LIVE MUSIC

45 ⭐ Map p86, B5

One of the city's largest concert venues hosts a range of big-name international stars. (www.oslospektrum.no; Sonja Henies plass 2; ▣Oslo Spektrum)

Shopping

Cappelens Forslag

BOOKS

46 🔒 Map p86, B5

Both a rare and cult lit dealer and cafe, this bookshop is set to be your new favourite. Make yourself at home on the front-room sofa with a good coffee and browse your way through its first editions and other gems, most of which are in English. It also hosts readings, book launches and concerts. (☏908 81 106; www.cappelensforslag.no; Bernt Ankers gate 4; ☽11am-6pm Mon-Fri, to 4pm Sat; ▣Brugata)

Ensemble

FASHION & ACCESSORIES

47 🔒 Map p86, B3

Clean by Christina Ledang (a stellar local stylist) might be one of the few Norwegian labels here, but there's still a particularly 'northern' sensibility on display at this pretty shop. Garments by Danish label Norse Projects hang above shoes by

Swedish shoemakers All Tomorrow's Parties, or find the racks of colourful cool Swede Rodebjer and lingerie and swimming costumes by Dutch darlings Love Stories. (☑414 60 566; http://ensemble.as; Nordre Gate 15; ☉11am-6pm Mon-Fri, 10am-5pm Sat & Sun; 🚋Schous plass)

Hevn
FASHION & ACCESSORIES

48 🔒 Map p86, B4

Nordic noir or Norwegian black, call it what you will. This shop specialises in the pared-back, mildly Gothic brand of Scandinavian fashion. There's both menswear and womens wear, jewellery and bags and shoes. All clothing is made ethically and it stocks a large range of designers from Norway, Sweden and Denmark. (☑400 62 430; https://hevn.no/; Torggata 36; ☉11am-7pm Mon-Sat; 🚋34)

Chillout Travel Centre
BOOKS

49 🔒 Map p86, B3

This is our kind of shop: good coffee, tasty dishes from around the world (dhal from India, snacks from Italy and cakes from...where else but Norway), loads of travel essentials such as bags and shoes, and a travel bookshop bursting with travel literature and guidebooks in Norwegian and English, including Lonely Planet guides. (☑22 35 42 00; www.chillout.no;

Markveien 55; ☉10am-7pm Mon-Sat, noon-6pm Sun; 🚋Schous plass)

Acne Studios Archive
FASHION & ACCESSORIES

50 🔒 Map p86, C4

The Swedish super-label has a handful of beautiful shops throughout Oslo, but this is the pick if you're after a bargain, with deep discounts on last year's stock. It's also worth a peek just for the beautiful photo murals of sculptor Gustav Vigeland's old studio. (☑22 60 93 00; www.acnestudios.com; Markveien 60; ☉11am-7pm Mon-Fri, to 6pm Sat & Sun; 🚋Schous plass)

Fransk Bazaar
VINTAGE

51 🔒 Map p86, B2

A local Francophile haunt run by a friendly Franco-Norwegian couple. Pour over the soulful French vintage homewares, objects and clothing in this delightfully jumbled and attractive shopfront. (www.franskbazar.no; Grünersgate 5; ☉noon-6pm Wed-Sat, 1-5pm Sun; 🚋Olaf Ryes plass)

Hasla
JEWELLERY

52 🔒 Map p86, C3

Norwegian silversmiths handcraft simple designs inspired by nature as well as classic Scandinavian modern pieces. (☑922 78 777; http://hasla.no; Markveien 54; ☉11am-6pm Mon-Fri, to 4pm Sat; 🚋Schous plass)

Typical building in Grünerløkka

Marita Stiftelsen
VINTAGE

53 🔒 Map p86, B4

Heaven for those who like to rummage for treasures, this bric-a-brac charity shop has shelves packed with vintage china, old lamps, glassware and coffee pots, with a smaller section upstairs for books and records. (📞22 38 19 20; http://marita.no; Markveien 67; ⏲11am-5pm; 🚇Biermanns gate)

Gulating Grünerløkka
ALCOHOL

54 🔒 Map p86, C3

Beer-lovers' heaven with one of Norway's largest selections of beers from classics to the novel and the rare. Friendly staff make it a double

pleasure. (📞958 42 611; www.facebook. com/GulatingOlutsalgGrunerlokka; Markveien 48; ⏲10am-8pm Tue-Fri, to 6pm Sat, noon-6pm Mon; 🚇Schous plass)

Vinmonopolet
WINE

55 🔒 Map p86, B3

This branch of the state wine and spirit chain has a good selection of French, Italian and Spanish wines, including well-priced French wine in plastic screw-cap bottles, excellent for picnicking by the river. Note: you must be least 20 years old to purchase, and there are usually long queues on Friday and Saturday afternoons. (www.vinmonopolet. no; Nordre gate 16; ⏲10am-6pm Mon-Thu, 9am-6pm Fri, 9am-3pm Sat; 🚇Schous plass)

FOTO5593/SHUTTERSTOCK ©

Explore

Sofienberg, Grønland & Tøyen

The city's eastside is one of contrasts. Long a solidly working-class en-clave, it's been transformed by both a large immigrant population and a continuing wave of gentrification over the last decade. Sofienberg is a quiet, green residential neighbourhood while Grønland and Tøyen, with their bars and smart bistros, are touted as the new Grünerløkka, if still gritty in parts (just the way the 'Tøyen baby' crew like it).

The Sights in a Day

These largely residential neighbourhoods hide away some of the city's most fascinating sights. Begin your day with a wander around **Ekebergparken** (p107), getting lost and stumbling upon a Louise Bourgeois or Jake and Dinos Chapman plonked in fields and forest dells.

In summer have lunch on the gloriously sited terrace of **Ekeberg Restaurant** (p109), while taking in the building's beautiful functionalist lines, then walk or tram it to the Botanical Garden for time with the stuffed Arctic animals of the **Natural History Museum** (p108). Cross the road to the wonderful Munch-dedicated **Munchmuseet** (p108).

An early dinner of Neo Nordic treats at **Brutus** (p109) beckons. Its rock-and-roll soundtrack will put you in the mood for some barhopping back down in Grønland.

For a local's day in the eastside, see p105.

 Local Life

Eastside Wandering (p105)

 Best of Oslo

Eating
Brutus (p109)

Olympen (p110)

Handwerk (p109)

Ekeberg Restaurant (p109)

Entertainment
Gloria Flames (p111)

Galleries
Munchmuseet (p108)

For Kids
Natural History Museum (p108)

Parks
Botanical Garden (p108)

Getting There

🚋 **Tram** 19 from Jernbanetorget (Central Station) goes to Ekebergparken.

🚆 **Train** Lines 1, 2, 3, 4 and 5 go to Tøyen.

Local Life
Eastside Wandering

Rapid gentrification has not taken the edge off Oslo's eastside, with its appeal still lying in its earthy, vibrant and historic streets. Grønland has long been a local's secret for cheap eats, edgy bars and late-night fun, with Tøyen, a little further on and still mainly residential, now becoming a culinary destination in its own right.

❶ Brown Pubs & Curry Night

Take in Oslo at its most multicultural and vibrant with a stroll along this busy strip, stopping for a lunchtime curry at **Punjab Tandoori** (☎22 17 20 86; www.punjabtandoori.no; Grønland-sleiret 24; lunch deal 80-90kr; mains 80-135kr; ⏱11am-11pm Mon-Sat, noon-10pm Sun; Ⓣ Grønland), a canteen-style affair serving spot-on northern Indian curries. Go for a cleansing ale at one of the street's many down and dirty brown pubs.

❷ Gallery Stop

An artist-run space, **1857** (☎22 17 60 50; http://1857.no; Tøyenbekken 12; ⏱noon-5pm Wed-Fri, to 4pm Sat & Sun; ⓣGrønland) popped up in a former lumberyard in 2010 and it's one of the city's most respected and enduring galleries. It's especially known for its collaborative curatorial efforts between young Norwegian artists and those from Europe and beyond. Openings are also some of the city's most fun.

❸ City Village

A picturesque detour brings you to **Kampen** (🚌60, ⓣTøyen), a residential neighbourhood that's retained its traditional, quintessentially Norwegian architecture. The stone Kampen Church is surrounded by streets of wooden houses, many of them painted in red and orange, that make it feel like another city entirely. It makes for a charming stroll any time of the year but is particularly lovely in autumn.

❹ Old Oslo

The site of the original city – **Gamlebyen** – now offers a glimpse of Oslo life in the 1800s, where Kampen-style wooden houses are replaced by apartments and heritage railway buildings. Beneath these there are still many traces of the city's medieval history and in **Middelalderparken** – the 'medieval park' – you can stroll around the ruins of St Clement's Church and cemetery that dates to around 1050.

❺ Tøyen, Baby

Although its streets of apartment buildings are satisfyingly grand and there's some pretty views from Størligata, there's not a lot to see in Tøyen. Stop by in the early evening for a drink or dinner at **Grådi** (☎978 80 544; www.facebook.com/gradirestaurantogbar; Sørligata 40; mains 90-140kr; ⏱11am-1am Tue-Sat, to midnight Sun; ⓣTøyen), an airy local's haunt with lovely neighbourhood views.

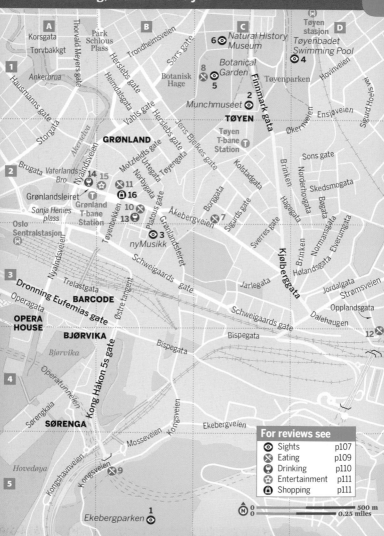

A
Korsgata
Torvbakkgt
Thorvald Meyers gate
Park
Schlous
Plass

B
Trondheimsveien
Herslebs gate
Sars gate

C
Natural History
Museum 6
Botanical
Garden
Botanisk
Hage
8
5

Tøyen
stasjon
Tøyenbadet
Swimming Pool
4 **D**
Hovinveien

1
Hausmanns gate
Ankerbrua
Heimdalsgata
Vahls gate
Finnmark gata
Tøyenparken
Ensjøveien
Sigurd Hoels vei

Storgata
Akerelva
Nylandsveien
GRØNLAND
Motzfeldts gate
Urtegata
Jens Bjelkes gate
Herslebs gate
Tøyengata
Munchmuseet 2
TØYEN
Tøyen
T-bane
Station
Økernveien
Brinken
Sons gate
Nordre høvgata
Skedsmogata
Bøgata
Normannsgata
Elverumgata

2
Brugata
Vaterlands
Bro
14
15
Grønlandsleiret
Grønland
T-bane
Station
Sonja Henies
plass
11
16
Norbygata
10
13
Plarous gate
Tøyenbekken
Grønlandsleiret
Åkebergveien
Borggata
7
Kolstadgata
Sigurds gate
Sverres gate
Hagegata
Brinken
Hølandsgata
Jarlegata
Normannsgata
Jordalgata
Strømsveien
Kjølberggata

Oslo
Sentralstasjon
3
nyMusikk
Schweigaards gate

3
Nylandsveien
Trelastgata
Dronning Eufemias gate
Operagata
BARCODE
Østre tangent
Schweigaards gate
Opplandsgata
Dalehaugen
12

**OPERA
HOUSE**
BJØRVIKA
Kong Håkon 5s gate
Bispegata
Bispegata

4
Bjørvika
Operatunnelen
Sørengkaia
SØRENGA
Kongsveien
Mosseveien
Kongsveien
Ekebergveien

Hovedøya
9
Kongshavnveien
Kongsveien
Ekebergparken 1

5

For reviews see	
⊙ Sights	p107
⊗ Eating	p109
☕ Drinking	p110
★ Entertainment	p111
🔒 Shopping	p111

N
0   500 m
0   0.25 miles

Munchmuseet (p108)

Sights

Ekebergparken

PARK

1  Map p106, B5

Ekebergparken has cemented Oslo's reputation as a contemporary-art capital and, in particular, one devoted to sculpture. A vast forested public park overlooking the city and the Oslofjord is dotted with work from the collection of property developer and art collector Christian Ringnes, with artists represented including Louise Bourgeois, Marina Abramović, Jenny Holzer, Tony Oursler, Sarah Lucas, Tony Cragg and Jake and Dinos Chapman, and a few traditional works from Rodin, Maillol and Vigeland.

You'll need at least half a day to explore properly, and expect your visit to unfold more as a treasure hunt than a usual museum experience. While seeking out the various installations, make sure you visit the **Ekeberg Stairs**, a historic as well as breathtaking viewpoint, and the **Munch Spot**, the view that inspired *The Scream* (as well as a 2013 Abramović work). There are children's activities held in the Swiss-chalet-style **Lund's House**, where you'll also find a museum exploring the geological and natural world of the park, as well as an art and design shop. (Ekeberg Sculpture Park; ☎21 42 19 19; https://ekebergparken. com; Kongsveien 23; admission free; ⏲24hr; 🚋Ekebergparken)

EVIKKA/SHUTTERSTOCK ©

Munchmuseet
GALLERY

2 Map p106, C1

A monographic museum dedicated to Norway's greatest artist Edvard Munch (1863–1944), and housing the largest collection of his work in the world: 28,000 items including 1100 paintings and 4500 watercolours, many of which were gifted to the city by Munch himself (although his best-known pieces, including *The Scream,* are held in the Nasjonalgalleriet (p24)).To get here, take a bus or the T-bane to Tøyen, followed by a 300m signposted walk. (Munch Museum; 23 49 35 00; www.munchmuseet.no; Tøyengata 53; adult/child 100kr/free; 10am-4pm, to 5pm mid-Jun–late Sep; T Tøyen)

nyMusikk
GALLERY

3 Map p106, B3

Part gallery, part office, part library and part performance space, nyMusikk hosts a program of sound-focused art shows, performances and festivals. Even if there's nothing on, staff are happy for you to come in and browse the music magazines and literature and to chat about what's going on in the city. (21 99 68 00; http://nymusikk.no/; Platous gate 18; office 10am-3pm; T Grønland)

Tøyenbadet Swimming Pool
SWIMMING

4 Map p106, D1

Near the Munch Museum, this complex has a mixture of large indoor pools and summer-only outdoor pools. The exact opening times for public swimming depends on the day and what lessons are running. (23 30 44 70; Helgesens gata 90; adult/child 98/48kr; 9am-7pm; T Tøyen)

Botanical Garden
GARDENS

5 Map p106, C1

Oslo's 6.5-hectare Botanical Garden – the oldest in Norway – has a beautiful woody arboretum, a sublime scent garden, a mini-mountain landscape and a collection of rare specimens from the Oslo fjords, including four that are almost extinct in nature. Look out also for the woven sculptures by British artist Tom Hare or just come for a walk, loll under a tree or grab a coffee from Handwerk (p109) cafe. (Botanisk Hage; Sars gate 1; admission free; 7am-9pm mid-Mar–Sep, to 5pm rest of year; T Tøyen)

Natural History Museum
MUSEUM

6 Map p106, C1

Under the trees of Oslo's Botanical Garden, the university's serious-looking Natural History Museum comprises two different collections: the Zoological Museum, which, as you might guess, is stuffed full of stuffed (excuse the pun) native wildlife; and the geological-palaeontological collection, which is closed for renovation until 2020. The admission fee also allows you to get green-fingered with the tropical plants inside the greenhouses. (Naturhistorisk Museum; www.nhm.uio.no; Sars gate 1; adult/child 50/25kr; 11am-4pm Tue-Sun; T Tøyen)

Eating

Brutus NEW NORDIC €€

7 Map p106, C2

With some of the biggest names in wine involved in this casual Tøyen corner spot, you could easily call Brutus a wine bar and not be wrong. But that would overlook that the cooking is some of the most exciting, and accessible, in the city. The space is pure Oslo: earthy, knowing, whimsical, rock and roll. (22 38 00 88; www.barbrutus. no; Eiriks gate 2; dishes 85-255kr, snacks 55-90kr; 5pm-1am; Munkegata)

Handwerk CAFE, BAKERY €

8 Map p106, C1

If you can't make it out into the countryside, come and find this beautiful cafe in the centre of the Botanical Garden. Set in a historic farm building, its pale-blue interior is lined with exquisite floral artworks, rows of candles and pendant lights. Windows reveal viridian (or snowy) views of the gardens all around while all is cosy within. (22 60 85 00; http://handwerk. no/Botaniske.html; Sarsgate 1; daily special 135-145kr, sandwiches 75kr; 10am-4pm; Tøyen)

Ekeberg Restaurant NORWEGIAN €€€

9 Map p106, B5

Lars Backer's early Oslofunkis (functionalist) masterpiece from 1929 fell into disrepair in the 1980s but happily is again here for all to enjoy, with a Neo Nordic dining room known for its simple, careful and elegant cooking. There's also a summertime eyrie terrace serving burgers, mussels and

---

Understand
Neo Nordic New Kids on the Block

For a while it seemed the Nordic cooking scene that the world had fallen in love with had passed Norway by, in the absence of a global superstar chef such as Copenhagen's René Redzepi or Swedish wildman Magnus Nilsson. Come to Oslo today, though, and you'll be spoilt for choice: globally renowned Michelin-starred places such as **Maaemo** (Map p106, B3; 22 17 99 69; https:// maaemo.no; Schweigaards gate 15; menu 2600kr; 6pm-midnight Wed & Thu, from noon Sat & Sun; Bussterminalen Grønland) and Kontrast (p88) have been joined by a startling number of boundary-pushing but highly accessible bistros serving up serious, sensual and supremely local food in good-times surrounds. These restaurants, such as Brutus and Pjoltergeist (p88), often employ a small plate approach, tend to throw something ironic or provocative on the stereo (most likely played on vinyl), and will have a sommelier who knows the people who produce the wine in Austria's Burgenland or Italy's Friuli by name.

Local Life
Multicultural Shopping

Bustling Grønlandsleiret is home to the city's most-loved Indian restaurant, Punjab Tandoori (p104), and there's plenty more spice to be found on this strip. Head to Grønland Bazaar or one of the many other Asian and Middle Eastern grocers for great-value picnic supplies.

fries, and prawn sandwiches. (☑23 24 23 00; www.ekebergrestauranten.com; Kongsveien 15; mains 295-310kr, set menu 650kr, terrace mains 170-190kr; ☉11am-midnight Mon-Sat, noon-10pm Sun; 🚋Ekebergparken)

Olympen   NORWEGIAN €€

12 Map p106, B2

Murals of the local streetscapes from the 1920s combine with dark wood panelling and chandeliers to make the easy-to-like, affordable Norwegian pub grub (steaks, suckling pig, mackerel) here something out of the ordinary. Known universally as Lompa, as a beer hall it also serves more than 100 beers, and is a beloved part of Grønland history. (☑24 10 19 99; www.olympen. no; Grønlandsleiret 15; mains 140-260kr; ☉11am-midnight Sun-Tue, to 1am Wed & Thu, to 3.30am Fri & Sat; ☐37)

Asylet   NORWEGIAN €€€

11 Map p106, B2

A classic hostelry dating from 1730 nestles in Grønland's multicultural heart. Head through the arch into

the cobbled courtyard, surrounded by wooden galleries, then head inside to the low-ceilinged, half-timbered pub, complete with flagstones, beams and a decidedly wonky-looking fireplace. The food is filling and traditional – it's particularly known for its *smørbrød* (open-faced sandwiches). (☑22 17 09 39; www.asylet.no; Grønland 28; mains 245-270kr; ☉11am-11.30pm Mon & Tue, to 12.30am Wed-Fri, noon-12.30am Sat to 10.30pm Sun; 🇹Grønland)

Smia Galleri   NORWEGIAN €€€

12 Map p106, D4

An old bakery has been transformed into a cosy candlelit space that serves posh Norwegian and international dishes. The leafy patio is perfect in summer and you can linger until midnight. Check the website for its jazz evenings too.It takes about 15 minutes to get here: from Oslo S, take bus 37 towards Helsfyr T-bane station and get off at Vålerenga. (☑22 19 59 20; Opplandsgata 19; mains 205-280kr; ☉2-10pm Tue-Fri, noon-10pm Sat & Sun; 🇹Grønland)

Drinking

Pigalle   CLUB, BAR

13 Map p106, B2

As unexpected as it might be in this street of grocers and curry places, Pigalle's latest incarnation feels like a set from an '80s Luc Besson movie, with an organic curved oak-veneer roof, a conservatory, palm trees, lots of black and green, and mirrors

FISHMAN/ULLSTEIN BILD VIA GETTY IMAGES ©

Dattera Til Hagen

☑ Top Tip

Dattera Til Hagen Music Fest

If you're in town during the summer music festival period and have missed out on tickets, check the dates for Dattera Til Hagen's great-value mini-festivals, which feature name live acts and DJs in its atmospheric courtyard.

Entertainment

Gloria Flames
LIVE MUSIC

15 ⭐ Map p106, B2

Gloria Flames is a popular rock bar hosting frequent gigs (including some big-name performers), and is home to a roof-terrace bar during daylight hours. (📞401 46 163; www.gloriaflames. no; Grønland 18; ☺4pm-3am Wed-Sun; Ⓣ Grønland)

galore. If you're lost, it's upstairs from the restaurant Olympen. (📞24 10 19 99; www.olympen.no; Grønlandsleiret 15; ☺4pm-1am Tue & Wed, to 3am Thu-Sat; 🚌37)

Dattera Til Hagen
BAR

14 🚇 Map p106, A2

A rambling, defiantly bohemian bar with a backyard beer garden that goes off in summer. DJs and live music make for even more lively days or nights. (www.dattera.no; Grønland 10; ☺11am-1am Mon-Wed, to 2am Thu, to 3.30am Fri & Sat, noon-midnight Sun; Ⓣ Grønland)

Shopping

Grønland Bazaar
SHOPPING CENTRE

16 🔒 Map p106, B2

A mostly Middle Eastern shopping centre, with a food court. (Tøyengata 2; ☺10am-8pm Mon-Sat; 🚌37)

Explore

St Olafs Plass, Bislett & St Hanshaugen

Off the tourist map, these neighbourhoods have a booming eating and drinking scene catering to their large population of students and young professionals. Whether you stick to the restaurants around St Olafs plass or venture as far as the hilly St Hanshaugen Park and Bislett Stadium, it's a lovely place to explore at leisure.

ANNA LEVAN/SHUTTERSTOCK ©

The Sights in a Day

☀️ Begin your day with an excellent espresso at **Fuglen** (p119) then explore the 18th-century enclave of red, rust and white painted wooden houses around **Damstredet** (p116), a tiny neighbourhood that still evokes an Oslo before industrialisation.

☀️ Next, get to know locals' favourite Ullevålsveien and the surrounding streets and have lunch at **Smalhans** (p118), or grab picnic supplies from **Baker Hansen** (p117) and **Gutta På Haugen** (p121) and head to rambling, vista-filled **St Hanshaugen Park** (p116)

🌙 Have another coffee at **Java Espressobar** (p121) or an afternoon wine and some cycling chat at **Rouleurs of Oslo** (p119). Then discover Oslo's hype-free fine-dining scene at beautiful neighbourhood favourite **Kolonialen** (p116), brought to you by a Maaemo alumni.

💜 Best of Oslo

Eating
Kolonialen (p116)

Kunstnernes Hus (p119)

Smalhans (p118)

Drinking
Fuglen (p119)

Rouleurs of Oslo (p119)

Fuglen (p119)

Java Espressobar (p121)

Shopping
Fuglen (p119)

Gutta På Haugen (p121)

For Kids
St Hanshaugen Park (p116)

Getting There

🚌 **Bus** 21 passes through St Hanshaugen on its route from Grünerløkka to Tjuvholmen.

🚊 **Tram** 13 and 19 are the closest city trams.

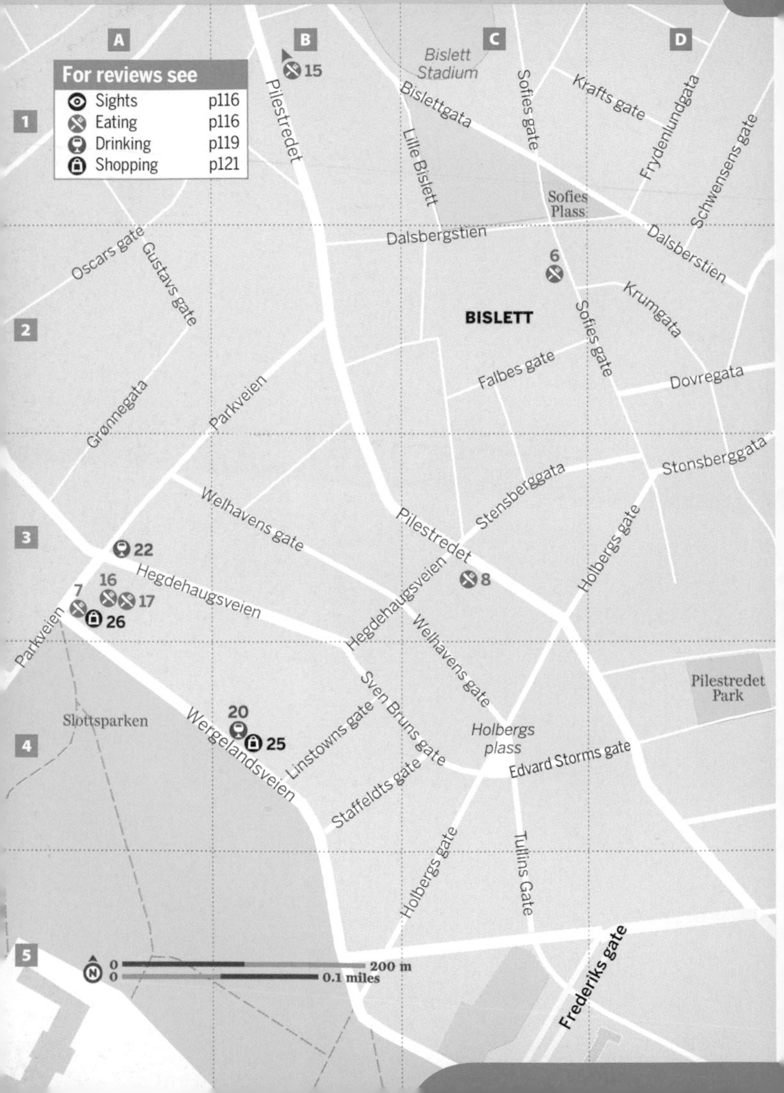

A

B

C

D

⊗ 15

Bislett
Stadium

Pilestredet

Bislettgata

Sofies gate

Krafts gate

Frydenlundgata

Schwensens gate

For reviews see

◎	Sights	p116
⊗	Eating	p116
⊕	Drinking	p119
⊕	Shopping	p121

1

Lille Bislett

Sofies
Plass

Dalsbergstien

Dalsberstien

Oscars gate

Gustavs gate

6
⊗

BISLETT

Krumgata

2

Grønnegata

Parkveien

Falbes gate

Sofies gate

Dovregata

Welhavens gate

Pilestredet

Stensberggata

Holbergs gate

Stonsberggata

3

⊕ 22

Hegdehaugsveien

16 ⊗⊗ 17

⊕ 26

⊗ 8

7
⊗⊕

Parkveien

Hegdehaugsveien

Welhavens gate

Pilestredet
Park

4

Slottsparken

Wergelandsveien

20
⊕
⊕ 25

Linstowns gate

Sven Bruns gate

Staffeldts gate

Holbergs
plass

Edvard Storms gate

Holbergs gate

Tullins Gate

Frederiks gate

5

N

0   200 m
0   0.1 miles

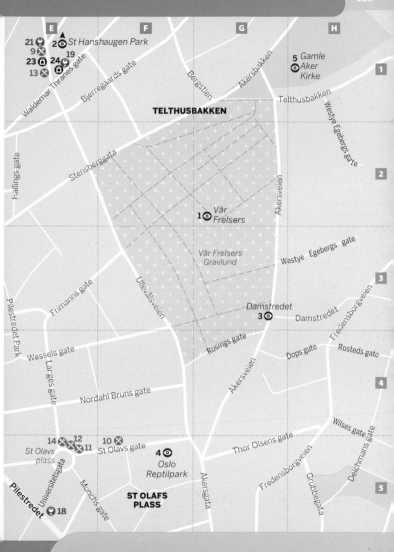

E **F** **G** **H**

21 ⬤
9 ✕
23 🔒 24 🔒
13 ✕

2 ⊙ St Hanshaugen Park
19

5 Gamle
⊙ Aker
Kirke

1

Waldemar Thranes gate

Bjerregaards gate

Bergsstien

Akersbakken

Telthusbakken

Westye Egebergs gate

TELTHUSBAKKEN

Fallings gate

Stensberggata

Akersveien

2

1 ⊙ Vår
Frelsers

Vår Frelsers
Gravlund

Westye Egebergs gate

3

Frimanns gate

Ullevålsveien

Damstredet
3 ⊙

Damstredet

Fredensborgveien

Pilestredet Park

Wessels gate

Rosings gate

Dops gate

Rosteds gate

4

Lars ges gate

Nordahl Bruns gate

Akersveien

Wilses gate

Deichmans gate

14 ✕ ✕ 12
11
St Olavs
plass

10 ✕
St Olavs gate

4 ⊙
Oslo
Reptilpark

Thor Olsens gate

Fredensborgveien

Grubbegata

5

Pilestredet

Universitetsgata

18

Munchs gate

**ST OLAFS
PLASS**

Akersgata

Sights

Vår Frelsers
CEMETERY

1 Map p114, G2

This triangular cemetery dates to the Napoleonic wars, but it's most notable as the final resting place of artist Munch and writer Ibsen. Ibsen's grand obelisk is marked with a hammer, while Munch's grave is graced by a bust of the artist. For Harry Hole fans, an apartment overlooking the cemetery (Ullevålsveien 15) is the site of a murder in *The Devil's Star*. (Æreslunden; Akersbakken 32; ⊙24hr; 🚌37)

St Hanshaugen Park
VIEWPOINT

2 Map p114, E1

This huge park is a locals' favourite and, from its top, a very pleasant place to get a view of the city. The neighbourhood's name – a reference to 'midsummer hill' – comes from the park, not the other way around, as it was a popular spot for midsummer bonfires. (Geitmyrsveien 31; 🚌37)

Damstredet
AREA

3 Map p114, G3

The quirky 18th-century wooden homes of the Damstredet district and the nearby Telthusbakken are a nice change of pace from the modern architecture of the city centre. Once an impoverished shanty town, Damstredet has become a popular residential neighbourhood for artists. To get there, walk north on Akersgata and turn right on Damstredet gate. Telthusbakken is a little further up Akersgata, also on the right. (🚌54)

Oslo Reptilpark
ZOO

4 Map p114, F5

For something slippery, most kids will love meeting the snakes and lizards (as well as the odd monkey) at the Oslo Reptilpark. (www.reptilpark.no; St Olavs gate 2; adult/child 115/85kr, with Oslo Pass free; ⊙10am-6pm Apr-Aug, Tue-Sun Sep-Mar; 🚌37)

Gamle Aker Kirke
CHURCH

5 Map p114, H1

This medieval stone church, located north of the centre on Akersbakken, dates from 1080 and is Oslo's oldest building. Take bus 37 from Jernbanetorget to Akersbakken, then walk up past the churchyard. (Akersbakken 26; ⊙noon-2pm Mon-Sat; 🚌37)

Eating

Kolonialen
GASTRONOMIC €€€

6 Map p114, C2

When a venture is led by the ex-Maaemo owner, you can guess the food will be extraordinary, and it is. The short menu is a mix of pan-European dishes done with a contemporary playfulness that stops short of quirky, care of the Australian chef. (📞401 03 578; www.kolonialenbislett.no; Sofiesgate 16; mains 240-290kr; 🚌37)

FISHMAN/ULLSTEIN BILD VIA GETTY IMAGES ©

Fuglen (p119)

Kafe Oslo

CAFE €€

7 Map p114, A3

Litteraturhuset is one of the state-run organisations dedicated to the arts and here it is all about the promotion of literature, with frequent workshops, talks and debates, not all of them in Norwegian. It's also a lovely place to come and rest weary feet, with a cafe and bar serving a menu of Norwegian soul food tasty enough to attract the odd princess from the neighbouring Royal Palace. (Litteraturhuset; ☑21 54 85 71; www.kafeoslo. no; Wergelandsveien 29; mains 155-245kr; ☼10am-12.30pm Mon-Thu, 10am-2pm Fri & Sat, noon-8pm Sun; 🚌17B)

Bislett Kebab House

KEBAB €

8 Map p114, C3

Spawning a chain of kebab shops all over Oslo, this is the original and is beloved by Oslo's students, past and present. (BKH; ☑22 46 80 44; https:// bislettkebabhouse.no; Hegdehaugsveien 2; kebab 65-125kr; ☼10am-3.30am; 🚌17B)

Baker Hansen

BAKERY €

9 Map p114, E1

The original of what's now a chain of Oslo and regional bakeries. Come here for old-school Norwegian baking made with care and affection. The stuffed cheese and ham wheat rolls are what every Norwegian remembers from picnics and parties, and the slices of fresh fruit-filled sponge and marzipan cake are timeless favourites, too. (☑94 02 32 30; www.bakerhansen.no; Ullevålsveien 45; snacks 39-159kr; ☼8am-7pm Mon-Fri, 9am-6pm Sat & Sun; 🚌37)

Izakaya Oslo

JAPANESE €

10 Map p114, F5

Bustling basement Japanese den that vibes Tokyo dive bar but is serious about both its food and Japanese liquors. Order up big from a short menu of authentic Japanese pub food, from salted soy beans to snack on while you sip a sake, beer or whisky, to dumplings, Korean pancakes and buckwheat noodle salads. (http:// izakayaoslo.com/; St Olavs gate 7; small plates 49-99kr; ☼5pm-1am Mon-Sat; 🚌37)

Bar Babylon
SUSHI, BAR €€

11 Map p114, E5

Hidden away behind Tekehtopa, Babylon may once have been a legendary nightclub but now is a respectable, if delightfully rambling, sushi restaurant and beer garden, filled with potted plants and vintage furniture and serving excellent sushi as well as *surøl*, the cultish sour beer. (☑47 97 80 89; www.tekehtopa.no; St Olavs plass 2; dishes 110-220kr, menu 750kr; ☉5pm-1am Mon-Thu, 4pm-3am Fri & Sat; ☐37)

Tekehtopa
ITALIAN €€

12 Map p114, E5

Part of the grand 1872 corner building housing Happolati and the once legendary nightclub, now sushi bar, Babylon, Tekehtopa is a lovely destination for catching evening rays on the summer terrace or cosying up under its beautiful ceiling murals come winter. The menu is contemporary Italian with daily pasta specials, risottos and arancini, *vitello tonnato* (cold-sliced veal with tuna sauce) and assorted fritters. (☑47 97 80 89; www.tekehtopa.no; St Olavs plass 2; mains 110-210kr; ☉11am-midnight Mon-Sat, noon-11pm Sun; ☐37)

Top Tip
Sofiesgate
Just below Bislett Stadium, Sofiesgate (Map p114, C1) and surrounds is a thriving, friendly eating and drinking enclave.

Smalhans
NORWEGIAN €€€

13 Map p114, E1

If you want to really capture the St Hanshaugen spirit, come to this busy restaurant-bar-cafe for its daily early meal – *husmannskost* – between 4pm and 6pm (175kr, though you can ask for a half portion) or its legendary big or small (*smalhans* = frugal, *krøsus* = cashed-up) dinners, where an ever-changing rota of rustic Norwegian dishes is served sharing-style. (☑22 69 60 00; www.smalhans.no; Ullevålsveien 43; 3-/6-course menu 450/650kr; ☉11am-1pm Tue-Sun; ☐37)

Happolati
ASIAN, GASTRONOMIC €€€

14 Map p114, E5

Oslo restaurateur Nevzat Arikan's latest offering has an extremely beautiful, highly crafted fit-out that speaks to both the contemporary Asian menu on offer and the beautiful, soulful and very Norwegian space it occupies. Calm as it all may be, there's a dynamism to the many small Japanese, Chinese and Southeast Asian–style dishes and to the super staff. (☑479 78 087; www.happolati.no; St Olavs plass 2; dishes 105-145kr, menu 650kr; ☉4.30-10pm Mon-Fri; ☐37)

L'ardoise
BAKERY, WINE BAR €€€

15 Map p114, B1

There's a concise traditional menu of French standards in the pretty dining room here for lunch and dinner, but it's the pastries – including the city's best croissants and some very credible macarons – that keep most of the

locals coming back. (☎22 11 09 65; www.
lardoise.no; Thereses gate 20; mains 225-295kr;
🕙11am-midnight Mon-Sat, to 6pm Sun; 🚌37)

Rust INTERNATIONAL €€

16 🍴 Map p114, A3

On a small side street lined with cafes
and restaurants, Rust is bright and
colourful. It has plenty of outdoor seat-
ing and loads of blankets for when it
gets cold. Great for a quiet beer, hearty
salads or stir-fries, burgers and ribs.
(☎23 62 65 05; www.rustoslo.com; Hegdehaugsveien 22; mains 95-169kr; 🕙11am-1am
Mon-Sat, noon-midnight Sun; 🚌17B)

Plah THAI €€€

17 🍴 Map p114, A3

Light and inventive Thai-inspired cuisine is the hallmark of this well-regard-
ed, very cool, intimate restaurant on a
quiet pedestrianised side alley close to
the Royal Palace. The place is split into
two parts: a restaurant, and a bar serving Southeast Asian street food–style
tapas. (☎22 56 43 00; www.plah.no; Hegdehaugsveien 22; 5 /9-course menu 545/625kr;
🕙5pm-1am Mon-Sat; 🚌17B)

Drinking

Fuglen COCKTAIL BAR, CAFE

18 🍷 Map p114, E5

Fuglen and its crew of merry, young
entrepreneurs are part of Oslo's dour-
to-dreamily cool reinvention. Since
taking over a traditional cafe, they've
launched a coffee and Norwegian
design mini-empire in Japan, while in
their home city they continue to roast
and brew as well as mix some of the
best cocktails around. (www.fuglen.com;
Universitetsgaten 2; 🕙7.30am-10pm Mon &
Tue, to 1am Wed & Thu, to 3am Fri, 11am-3am
Sat, to 10pm Sun; 🚌17B)

Rouleurs of Oslo WINE BAR, CAFE

19 🍷 Map p114, E1

An elegant Francophile of a bar that
happens also to be part of a bike-
repair workshop? Hello St Hanshaugen. Come here for daytime coffees
(and bike repairs), or in the evening
for a pre-dinner cocktail or Chablis. If
you don't want to leave (the wine list
is that good), don't, and make a meal
of its duck rillettes, pâté or charcuterie plates. (http://rosl.no; Ullevålsveien
16; 🕙noon-1am Mon-Thu, to 2am Fri & Sat, to
12.30am Sun; 🚌37)

Kunstnernes Hus BAR, PIZZA

20 🍷 Map p114, B4

One of the city's various artist-run
cultural institutions, Kunstnernes Hus
is set in a spectacular 1929 functionalist building with a broad terrace
overlooking the green of Slottsparken.
It's a supremely laid-back and scenic
place to have a spritz, wine or beer;
the crowd is an interesting mix of the
city's creatives; and there are always
excellent tunes playing on the decks.
(☎22 85 34 10; http://kunstnerneshus.no;
Wergelandsveien 17; 🕙11am-10pm Tue-Thu, to
3am Fri, noon-3am Sat, noon-8pm Sun; 🚌17B)

Understand

Nature City

The Norwegian term *friluftsliv* is both hard to say and hard to translate, but not difficult to understand once you've spent any time in the company of Norwegians. Coined in 1859 as the country urged itself onto independence, and popularised in a poem by Henrik Ibsen called 'Paa Vidderne' (On the Heights), its literal meaning is 'free air life'. In practice the word conjures a broad, quasi-spiritual sense of rightness in the outdoors. Oslo may be a rapidly growing urban metropolis, but it's also one of the world's most green cities, and blessed to be surrounded by spectacular waterways and mountains of its own. For locals here, the quest to spend time in the natural world is a priority above all others.

Fjordlife

Oslofjord's Hovedøya island feels deliciously remote with a landscape of rocky outcrops, forests and beaches. Its unique geology means it has plant specimens that are not found elsewhere in Norway, lovely beaches and walking paths. South of Hovedøya lies the undeveloped island of Langøyene, which has superb swimming from rocky or sandy beaches (one on the southeastern shore is designated for nude bathing). Waterbirds breed between the grassy islands of Gressholmen, Rambergøya and Heggholmen, and you can swim along Gressholmen's east coast.

Forests for Days

Northern Oslo is made up of huge swaths of pristine pine forest known as Nordmarka, an area which can be reached in 20 to 30 minutes on the city's T-bane and surely must be the largest, wildest backyard of any European city. More than 1200km of hiking trails draw locals in number in summer, as does the lure of fishing on Sognsvann lake. In winter there's both nordic skiing and downhill, snowshoeing and ski-jumping competitions – the locals just jump on the T-bane with their skis.

City Nature

Even in the heart of the city, the Akerselva, while lined with old industrial buildings and new developments, has stretches of quite wild beauty, with cascading falls, swimming holes and forested banks. Ekebergparken's rambling reaches too are full of geological wonders, wildflower-dotted pastures and surprisingly dense forests of pine, ash, black alder, maple, sallow and fir. Keen birdwatchers will notice woodpeckers, robins, blackbirds and different tits, and magnificent roe deer often appear.

Java Espressobar
CAFE

21 📍 Map p114, E1

Even if you're not in the neighbourhood, if you're a coffee fanatic it's worth the trip to pay homage to Java, which along with Tim Wendelboe and Fuglen revolutionised coffee in Norway. It's also a lovely light and high-ceilinged space to linger. (http://javaoslo.no; Ullevålsveien 47; ⏰7am-6pm Mon-Fri, from 8am Sat, from 9am Sun; 🚃37)

Lorry
BEER GARDEN, PUB

22 📍 Map p114, A3

There's nothing Neo Nordic about Lorry: just ask the fictional Harry Hole of the Jo Nesbø detective novels. But it's a great place for an atmospheric old-school beer either inside or out, and you can, of course, make like Harry and eat here, with a menu of traditional Norwegian favourites. (http://lorry.no; Parkveien 12; ⏰11am-1am Mon, to 3.30am Tue-Sat, noon-1am Sun; 🚃17B)

Shopping

Gutta På Haugen
FOOD & DRINKS

23 🔒 Map p114, E1

For picnic or self-catering supplies, head to this well-stocked St Hanshaugen institution. There's a huge cheese selection with both Norwegian and European produce, a lovely array of local sausages and boxes of the must-try Norwegian flat bread. Its fresh produce is the best of the season and

you can grab an excellent soft serve to take away at its ice-cream van across the road. (📞22 60 85 12; http://gutta.no/; Ullevålsveien 45; ⏰8am-7pm; 🚃37)

Fara
SPORTS & OUTDOORS

24 🔒 Map p114, E1

Nordic minimalist design and Norwegian endurance (they're fjord-proof, we're told) combine in this new cycle design outfit from Stjordal up north. Part of Rouleurs (p119) next door, cycling devotees will like to check these beauties out. You can also ask about its program of local rides. (www.rosl.no; Ullevålsveien 16; ⏰11-7pm Mon-Sat; 🚃37)

Torpedo
BOOKS

25 🔒 Map p114, B4

An Oslo-based art publisher that stocks both its own publications as well as other Norwegian and international art books and journals. It also organises artist book-based shows at Kunsthall Oslo. (www.torpedobok.no; Wergelandsveien 17; ⏰11am-4pm Tue & Wed, to 6pm Thu & Fri, noon-6pm Sat & Sun; 🚃Bjørvika)

Tanum Bookshop
CULTURAL CENTRE

26 🔒 Map p114, A3

Litteraturhuset's well-stocked bookshop is testament to the vibrancy of Norwegian publishing; it's a great place to pick up beautiful local children's books too. (Litteraturhuset; 📞23 69 10 80; http://litteraturhuset.no/no/huset/bokhandel/; Wergelandsveien 29; ⏰11am-8pm Mon-Fri, 10am-5pm Sat, noon-4pm Sun; 🚃17B)

Local Life
Day-tripping to Fredrikstad

Fredrikstad was once a hugely important trading centre between mainland Europe and western Scandinavia, and is home to one of the best-preserved, and prettiest, fortress towns in Scandinavia. The timbered houses, moats, gates and drawbridge of the Fredrikstad Gamlebyen – 'old town' – are simply enchanting. Around 90 minutes from Oslo, it's a relaxing and historic place for a day out of town.

Getting There

🚌 Intercity buses connect to the Fredrikstad Rutebilstasjon at the train station. Regular **Flybussekspressen** (www. flybussekspressen.no) services go from Fredrikstad to Oslo airport (307kr, 2¼ hours).

🚌 Fredrikstad is on the **NSB** (www.nsb.no) rail line between Oslo and Göteborg. Trains run daily to/from Oslo (221kr, one hour); reserve seats.

🚗 By car, follow the E6 south out of Oslo. Just after Råde, turn south on the 110 and follow it to Fredrikstad.

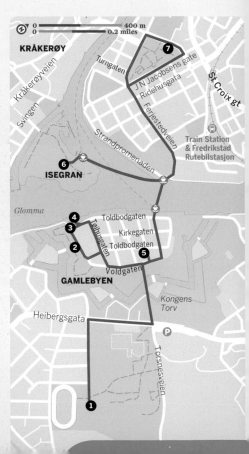

❶ Gallows Hill

Begin your exploration with a bird's-eye view from what was once called 'Gallows Hill'. Here stands the flower-festooned **Kongsten Festning**, dating from 1685; it once served as a lookout and warning post for the troops at Gamlebyen below. Scramble around the turrets, embankments, walls and stockade, or just laze in the sun and soak up the quiet.

❷ Museum

The **Fredrikstad Museum** (www.ostfoldmuseet.no; Tøihusgaten 41; adult/child 75/30kr; ⏱noon-4pm mid-Jun–late Aug, noon-3pm rest of year) is housed in a building dating back to 1776 and has scale models of the old town and an interesting collection of relics from three centuries of Fredrikstad's civilian, military and industrial activities, as well as a small military museum.

❸ Old Convict Prison

Among the finest old buildings in town, look out for the old **convict prison** (Salveriet), built in 1731.

❹ Bastion 5

This beautiful **Bastion 5** (Toldbodgaten 105), built between 1674 and 1691, is one of the oldest buildings in Gamlebyen and now is an arts centre and has a ceramics workshop and showroom to peruse.

❺ Slow Norwegian

Rustic **Majoren's Stue og Kro** (☎69 32 15 55; www.majoren.no; Voldportgata 73, Gamlebyen; mains 165-199kr; ⏱noon-8pm Mon-Thu, to 9pm Fri & Sat, to 7pm Sun) is loved by locals for its *koselig* (cosy) and historic atmosphere. Settle into the formal dining room for traditional stews served with cabbage, fried onions and boiled potatoes or steaks with root vegetables and spiced butter, or head to the garden for burgers and seafood salads.

❻ Across to the Islet

Norse sagas mention the 13th-century fortress of **Isegran** (www.isegran.no; with Fredrikstad Museum adult/child 75/30kr, ⏱noon-4pm Fri-Sun mid-Jun–late Aug), an islet in the Glomma that became a further line of defence against Sweden in the mid-17th century. The ruins of a stone tower are visible at the eastern end of the island. It's also the site of a small museum on local boatbuilding (from the time when boats were lovingly handcrafted from wood). By road or on foot, access is from Rv108, about 600m south of Fredrikstad city centre.

❼ Cathedral

Fredrikstad's 1880 cathedral reflects the town's 19th-century importance with its stained-glass work by Emanuel Vigeland. Norwegian practicality combines here with its piousness: bizarrely, the steeple contains a lighthouse, which still functions to steer ships up the sound.

The Best of
Oslo

Oslo Opera House (p48)
NANISIMOVA/GETTY IMAGES ©

Best Walks
All Along the Waterfront

🏃 The Walk

Once a heavily industrialised port area, Oslo's waterfront has been totally transformed over the last 20 years and is still in the process of rapid change. It makes for a heady mix of the new and the historic and the industrial and the natural.

Start Ekebergparken

Finish Astrup Fearney Museet

Length 4.5km; 2.5 hours

🍴 Take a Break

This route is lined with excellent places to eat but the top picks are the airy terrace of historic Ekeberg Restaurant (p109) and the prime waterfront stools at Vingen (p60) at the Astrup Fearnley Museet, at each end of the walk.

VALERY BARETA/SHUTTERSTOCK ©

View of Oslo's waterfront from Oslo Opera House

❶ Ekebergparken

For some of the best city views this side of Holmenkollen, begin your walk at **Ekebergparken** (p107). You'll also stroll past one of Norway's best contemporary-art collections, spying a Dan Graham or a Damien Hirst in between forests and fields.

❷ Bjørvika Views

Heading down towards the city, the fascinating Bjørvika lies before you, the former port in the throes of a massive overhaul. Past the cranes and building works lies the towers of Barcode, where the controversial project began, while along Sørengkaia is a new residential neighbourhood and swimming zone.

❸ Oslo Opera House

Oslo's most iconic **building** (p48) needs little introduction. A walk on the luminous marble roof for stunning 360-degree views of the city and Oslofjord is an absolute must, as is a poke around its soaring wooden interiors.

❹ Akerhusstranda

On a sunny day this stretch of road makes for a nice waterfront stroll (on a cold or wet one it can, admittedly, be a little bleak), with the fortress looming above and some evocative remnants of the old port still dotted along this strip.

❺ Pipervika

Oslo passenger ferries all dock here and there's little to remind you that this was once a fishing port, except for this charming **seafood restaurant** (p60), where you can eat this morning's catch straight from the boats, and which is named for the bay on which it stands.

❻ Astrup Fearnley Museet

The city's most-visited stretch of waterfront has a bustling boardwalk full of restaurants and ice-cream stands, bars and boats. Its mix-and-match contemporary architecture gives way to the serene sails of Renzo Piano's **Astrup Fearnley Museet** (p52) as you reach its island tip at Tjuvholmen.

Best Walks
Ibsen & Munch's Oslo

🏃 The Walk

The two great figures of Norwegian letters and art, Henrik Ibsen and Edvard Munch respectively, were both Oslo residents in the late 19th century. The city that inspired them to create some of the world's most insightful plays and some of its most chilling, disturbing paintings is still very much present.

Start Ibsen Museet

Finish Munchmuseet

Length 6km; three hours

✖ Take a Break

Grab a coffee at cafe-record store Hendrix Ibsen (p96), a typically Norwegian and irreverent homage to Ibsen (as well as to Jimi Hendrix, obviously).

JORG GREUEL/GETTY IMAGES ©

Henrik Ibsen statue

❶ Ibsen Museet

Not just a museum but Henrik Ibsen and his wife Suzannah's **home** (p34) from 1895 to 1906. Restored with period decor, Ibsen's study looks just as he left it.

❷ Ibsen Sitat

Ibsen's route from his home, the Ibsen Museet, to the Grand Café is marked out in pithy Ibsen quotes embedded in the footpaths.

❸ Nationaltheatret

Ibsen's *An Enemy of the People* was one of the inaugural plays performed when the Henrik Bull–designed **theatre** (p44) opened in 1899. The theatre is considered the home of Ibsen, with all of his works having been produced here.

❹ Grand Café

Every day for nine years, Ibsen walked from his home to the **Grand Café** (p37) for lunch and an evening drink, punctually at his special table in the cafe or Palm Garden between 1.20pm and 2pm, then from 6pm to 7.30pm. You can still order his favourite tipple, a *pjolter* (whisky and soda).

❺ Vår Frelsers Cemetery

Between Akersbakken, Akersveien and Ullevålsveien you'll find the **final resting place** (p116) of both Munch and Ibsen. Ibsen's obelisk is engraved with a hammer, while Munch's

is topped with a rather austere bust of the artist.

❻ Munch's Grünerløkka

Munch spent much of his childhood in this once working-class neighbourhood. You can't visit any of his apartments but you can wander past Fossveien 7, the home where his sister Sofie died and which inspired the painting *Death in the*

Sick Room, as well as Schous plass 1 where he later painted *The Sick Child.*

❼ Munchmuseet

End at Munch's own **museum** (p108), with its staggering collection of works – more than half of the artist's paintings and at least one copy of all his prints – mostly donated by Munch himself.

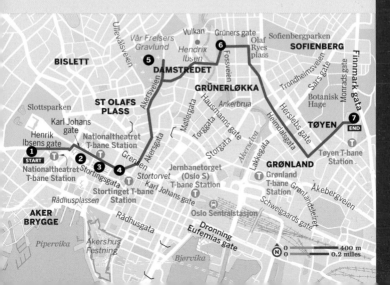

Best
Eating

MORTEN FALCH SORTLAND/GETTY IMAGES ©

Oslo's food scene has come into its own in recent years, attracting curious culinary-minded travellers who've eaten their way through Copenhagen and Stockholm and are looking for new sensations. Dining out in Oslo can involve a Michelin-starred restaurant, a hot-dog stand, peel-and-eat shrimp, a bar doing innovative Neo Nordic small plates, a super-traditional dining room or eateries doing convincingly authentic Japanese, Italian, French, Indian and Mexican dishes.

Neo Nordic Love

Traditional dishes are done with a twist: heritage ingredients (chicken hearts, cod tongue, blood sausage, slow-cooked beets, fresh cheese, rhubarb, barley) feature heavily. They're not exclusively Norwegian, so often incorporate Icelandic, Danish or other culinary elements.

Pizza Queens

Norway is known for its love of frozen pizza, though in Oslo expect proper Neapolitan or thin-crust pizza made with top-quality ingredients.

Upmarket Japanese

With some of the freshest fish in the world, sushi is big in Oslo. *Omakase* – a chef's choice degustation – is how cashed-up locals currently like to do it.

Best Neo Nordic

Maaemo Exquisite, poetic and innovative multicourse dinners at the country's best restaurant. (p109)

Brutus Serious attention to detail, pan-Nordic influences and natural wine. (p109)

Bass Low-key local with a simple but serious menu and a great interior. (p88)

Sentralen Restaurant Fabulous setting, friendly staff and superbly realised dishes. (p37)

Pjoltergeist Icelandic-Korean fusion in a re-imagined dive-bar. (p88)

Smalhans Set menus that draw legions of locals. (p118)

Grand Café (p37)

Kolonialen Maaemo-level food in a smart neighbourhood haunt. (p116)

Best Traditional Norwegian

Grand Café Henrik Ibsen's favourite; polished elegant cooking. (p37)

Olympen All the protein-heavy Norwegian favourites with a few contemporary surprises. (p110)

Theatercafeen Not entirely trad but still the place to go for a fish soup or langoustine and mayo. (p41)

Syverkiosken *Pølse* (hot-dog) heaven with traditional potato bread wrappings and all the trappings. (p89)

Best Pizza

Sentralen Cafeteria Evening pizza on incredible sourdough crusts. (p39)

Villa Paradiso There are always queues at this Grünerløkka legend. (p90)

Kunstnernes Hus Parkside pizza with Oslo's art scene. (p119)

Best Burgers

Munchies Perpetually busy Grünerløkka favourite. (p90)

Wünderburger Lofoten beef and build your own burgers. (p90)

Illegal Burgers Char-grilled patties and great fries. (p40)

Best
Bars & Cafes

LIISA LEESMENT/EYEEM/GETTY IMAGES ©

Oslo has a staggering choice of bars and pubs, from rowdy old boozers to venues serving the world's best wines. For those wanting a caffeine buzz instead, Oslo's Tim Wendelboe is one of the world's biggest names in coffee, and over the last decade he's been joined by a number of superior roasters and baristas. Before that, of course, coffee came filtered, black and in a large mug, and that's the way many Norwegians still like it.

Bar Zones

The city's most lively strip is around Grüner-løkka's Thorvald Meyers gate and the Torggata strip after the bridge across the Akerselva. The Youngstorget area has some of the most popular places close in the city centre, while the developments around Aker Brygge have brought more after-dark life to the waterfront. Grønland and Tøyen have an alternative feel, and St Hanshaugen has a nice collection of low-key, quietly cool places around Ullevålsveien.

Playtime

Communal games are a large part of Norwegian nightlife. Locals admit it's down to their reserved nature – the games are there to give them something to focus their attention on until the wine, beer or cocktails provide the desired level of disinhibition needed for small talk.

Best Cocktails

Torggata Botaniske Lush plant-filled bar with on-site herb garden. (p94)

Fuglen Neo Nordic twists using unusual liquors and foraged ingredients. (p119)

Vingen Fresh and innovative drinks list in a stunning waterfront location. (p60)

Himkok Cocktails on tap, literally. (p43)

Bettola Best Negronis in Oslo, along with great midcentury decor. (p96)

Best Wine Bars

Territoriet *The* wine-by-the-glass specialists, with literally hundreds to choose from. (p94)

Rouleurs of Oslo Beautiful homage to France

Fuglen (p119)

and Italy's most interesting producers. (p119)

Champagneria Fizzies from France, Italy and Spain (with tapas) in Frogner. (p78)

Dr Kneipp's Vinbar Long-time wine-lover's favourite with excellent casual plates, too. (p90)

Best Beer

Grünerløkka Brygghus Legendary microbrewery with everything from pilsners to *Weißbier*, Christmas beer and sours. (p96)

Røør Vinyl, vending machine snacks and more than 70 beers on tap. (p44)

Crowbar & Brewery In-house brews and a great selection of Norwegian beers on tap, all under the sign of the crow. (p95)

Best Bars with Games

Kulturhuset One of the city's most beautiful (and busy) shuffleboard rooms. (p42)

Oslo Camping Minigolf anyone? Drunk Norwegians, iron sticks, small hard balls: what could possibly go wrong? (p44)

Mir When everyone else was playing team sports, the kids at Mir were doing interpretive dance. (p94)

Paul's Boutique Ping-pong and hip-hop pair at this most laid-back of neighbourhood hangs. (p85)

Best Cafes

Tim Wendelboe A corner cafe with incredible coffee cred. Just go. (p94)

Supreme Roastworks Roasters out the back, friendly baristas at the front. (p85)

Handwerk Filter coffee only here; it's the bomb and made from some of the city's best beans. (p109)

Fuglen A gorgeous makeover of an original '60s cafe-bar; superb coffee and service. (p119)

Java Espressobar St Hanshaugen stalwart with great coffee in a lovely light space. (p121)

Hendrix Ibsen Good coffee, vinyl and healthy snacks by the river. (p96)

Best
Shopping

The city's Kirkegata, Nedre Slottsgate and Prinsens gate are home to a well-considered collection of Scandinavian and international fashion and homewares shops, with Frogner and St Hanshaugen also having good upmarket choices too. Head to Grünerløkka for vintage and Scandinavian fashion.

ROUTE66/SHUTTERSTOCK ©

Best Norwegian Design

Utopia Retro Modern One of the city's best vintage collections. (p78)

Fuglen This cafe and cocktail bar also deals in fabulous Norwegian vintage and reissued pieces. (p119)

FWSS Flagship of Norway's homegrown purveyor of Scandi style. (p46)

Norwegian Rain Bergen's finest high-fashion all-weather wear. (p45)

Ensemble Lovely curated fashion selection that features local designers. (p99)

Best Food & Drink

Gutta På Haugen Treasure trove of incredible Norwegian produce, plus imported cheese, charcuterie and deli goods. (p121)

Gulating Grünerløkka Norway's largest selection of beers. (p101)

Vinmonopolet Literally the *only* place to buy wine in Oslo. (p101)

Best Books & Records

Cappelens Forslag Cult lit and first editions, many in English. (p99)

Tronsmo Local literary hang-out with good selection of English-language books, a packed LGBT section and basement comics. (p45)

Nomaden Guides, maps and the rest, plus travel-savvy staff. (p78)

Best
Architecture

As the fastest-growing European capital, Oslo's built environment is a rapidly changing one, with iconic buildings springing up and newly redeveloped industrial areas like Bjørvika and Aker Brygge joining its interesting 17th-century streetscapes, 19th-century boom-town strips and 20th-century functionalist (aka 'Oslofunkis) gems.

B.AA. SÆTRENES/GETTY IMAGES ©

Best Historic Sites

Akershus Slott Renaissance palace with decidedly Medieval dungeons. (p36)

Oslo Cathedral This lovely baroque church also features a modernist mural and stained glass by Emanuel Vigeland. (p35)

Norsk Folkemuseum Explore different eras of Norwegian vernacular architecture in one sprawling park. (p58)

Royal Palace A pale-yellow stuccoed brick and notably pared-back neoclassical design. (p28)

Ibsen Museet A rare peek into domestic architecture of the late 19th-century, care of the country's most famous playwright. (p34)

Best 20th-Century Buildings

Rådhus Beautiful if bombastic late-functionalist building and interiors. (p36)

Internasjonalen Cold War–themed bar at the bottom of a classic Oslofunkis building. (p31)

Ekeberg Restaurant A stunning early funkis gem in a gorgeous setting. (p109)

Best Contemporary Architecture

Oslo Opera House Oslo-based architectural firm Snøhetta made their mark with this stunning waterfront work. (p48)

Astrup Fearnley Museet A statement Renzo Piano building that reflects its former dockside site. (p52)

The Thief Dark glamour lies within the city's most sought-after design hotel, care of Mellbye Architects. (p145)

Sentralen Fabulous fresh refit of an old bank HQ with a clever mash of contemporary and 19th-century elements. (p30)

Holmenkollen Ski Jump This dynamic curve of aluminium and glass jutting into the sky was designed by Julien de Smedt Architects in 2011. (p80)

Best
Museums &
Galleries

Oslo's museum offerings are up there with those of cities four times its size, with a fantastic range of beautifully tended institutions to spend days poring over. Most are clustered in the city centre, and there's a number on the Bygdøy Peninsula too. Private art collections, commercial galleries, and fascinating and intimate house museums join the big institutional players.

Museum Peninsula

Bygdøy has a number of museums scattered all about the peninsula, and there is never more than a very pleasant stroll between them. If you're not up for walking, or fancy a bit more ferry time, you can hop between the Vikingskipshuset wharf and that of the Maritime Museum.

Gallery-Hopping

You'll find a good number of the city's edgier art spaces in Grünerløkka (along with its art school, dance school and many of its creative-industry offices) and another cluster in nearby Grønland.

On the Horizon

More than ten years ago, the city's Nasjonalgalleriet, its contemporary art Museet for Samtidskunstfour, the Museum of Design and Decorative Arts and the Museum of Architecture merged and began the transition to an all-arts Nasjonalmuseet. Sitting by the Rådhus, and slated to open in 2020, the supermuseum will create a natural bridge between the new waterfront areas and the established city.

CINEMATOGRAPHER/SHUTTERSTOCK ©

Best Art Museums

Nasjonalgalleriet
Edvard Munch's *The Scream* plus the nation's largest collection of traditional and modern art. (p24)

Astrup Fearnley Museet Superstar-filled contemporary collection in a Renzo Piano building. (pictured; p52)

Munchmuseet A huge collection of Munch's work all under one roof. (p108)

IZZET KERIBA/GETTY IMAGES ©

Vikingskipshuset (p54)

Best Galleries

Rod Bianco Boundary-pushing work from both Norwegian and international contemporary artists, including hometown bad boy Bjarne Melgaard. (p85)

Standard Oslo art darling Matias Faldbakken shows at this edgy two-room space. (p87)

vi, vii Shows up-and-coming local artists in a 1930s building. (p35)

Best Museums for Norwegian Culture

Vikingskipshuset Just three ships, but so much and such great history. (p54)

Norwegian Maritime Museum Norway's rich maritime history explored in a beautiful Oslofjord setting. (p58)

Ibsen Museet A brilliant insight into the life and work one of the world's best playwrights. (p34)

Worth A Trip

The private **Henie-Onstad Art Centre** (Henie-Onstad Kunstsenter; ☎67 84 48 80; www.hok.no; Høvikodden; adult/child 100kr/free; ⏰11am-5pm Tue-Sun; 🚌Blommenholm) contains works by Joan Miró and Pablo Picasso, and assorted impressionist, abstract, expressionist and contemporary Norwegian works. It hosts big-name temporary contemporary shows too, and is just a 15-minute drive from the centre, or you can take bus 160 to Høvikodden from the Oslo Bus Terminal.

Best
Entertainment

Oslo's live-music scene is the envy of far larger cities, with gigs happening most nights and year-round. Venues are spread across the city but cluster in Vulkan, Grünerløkka and Grønland. World-class opera, ballet performances and classical music are also well represented, as is contemporary dance.

ROBIN NIEUWENKAMP/SHUTTERSTOCK ©

Best Intimate Live Music

Kafe Hærverk Oslo's most interesting live electronic and indie acts, plus great drinks. (p85)

Blå Legendary club for hip-hop, jazz, big bands, electronica and everything in between. (p98)

Revolver Great little band room with local and international acts most nights. (p98)

Gloria Flames Classic rock club. (p111)

Best Big-Name Live Music

Parkteatret Local and international acts in an old theatre in a great Grünerløkka location. (p98)

Rockefeller Music Hall The city's premier live venue for touring acts. (p98)

Oslo Spektrum Large venue for international acts. (p99)

Best Dance Venues

Blå Famous for its varied club nights. (p98)

Kafe Hærverk Best live electronica. (p85)

Mono A band venue that has electronica nights too. (p31)

Best Classical & Performance

Oslo Opera House A stunning venue for opera or ballet. (p48)

Nationaltheatret Theatre and musical performances. (pictured; p44)

Best
For Kids

Oslo is a wonderfully family-friendly destination, with hotels, restaurants and sights all giving a warm welcome to little travellers. Most Oslo parents will tell you the best activities are often the simplest and are free, and there are plenty of these, too.

NENAD NEDOMACKI/SHUTTERSTOCK ©

Best Museums

Vikingskipshuset Reconstructed Viking ships at the Viking Ship Museum. (p54)

Kon-Tiki Museum Guaranteed to inspire the inner explorer. (p59)

Natural History Museum Stuffed with stuffed Arctic wildlife, and has tropical greenhouses. (p108)

Akershus Festning Cannons and fortifications are always great for sparking the imagination. (p26)

Norsk Folkemuseum Lots of chances to play house; weekend and holiday events are geared towards children. (p58)

Best Outdoors

Frognerparken There are no rules against climbing the statues here or chasing your siblings around the garden's 3000m mosaic labyrinth. (p70)

St Hanshaugen Park Sprawling park with views in a very family-focused neighbourhood. (p116)

Tjuvholmen City Beach Oslofjord paddling for the little ones; stunning contemporary sculpture for you. (pictured; p59)

Best Eats

Villa Paradiso Pizza always pleases; this is beloved of local families and opens early. (p90)

Baker Hansen All the kid-friendly favourites, from cinnamon buns and cream-filled sponges to cheese and salad rolls. (p117)

Mathallen Oslo Everyone gets their pick at this

☑ Top Tips

▶ Well-vetted babysitters can be hired through Barnepasseren (www.barne passeren.no).

▶ Most museums will make you use their own baby carriages, so time your visit to start before sleep times.

happy food-hall's outlet. (p89)

Munchies Friendly neighbourhood burger bar. (p90)

Sentralen Cafeteria The Stokke high chairs are ready; come for great coffee, all-day salads or early-evening pizza. (p39)

Best
For Free

Oslo is an incredibly expensive city and museum prices can put a dent in a traveller's budget, even with a tourist pass. It does, however, have a few things that will cost you no krone at all.

MORTEN FALCH SORTLAND/GETTY IMAGES ©

Head to the Hills

Northern Oslo consists of huge areas of pristine pine forest known as Nordmarka, and surely must be the largest, wildest backyard of any European city. More than 1200km of hiking trails draw locals in numbers during the summer. Pick some blueberries, spot elks and go skinny-dipping.

Fjordlife

The Oslofjord is dotted with islands that are lovely to explore, including the undeveloped island of Langøyene, which has superb swimming from rocky or sandy beaches and where free camping is permitted.

☑ Top Tips

▶ Ferries to the Oslofjord islands sail from Vippetangen Quay and many are covered within the city zone travel pass.

▶ Nordmarka can easily be reached by on the city's T-bane.

Akershus Festning
Explore this medieval fortress and prepare for incredible views over the city and Oslofjord. (p26)

Oslo Opera House
Wander up and over the roof, take in the view, and explore the modern interior. (p48)

Rådhus An architectural landmark with incredible mid-century artwork. (p36)

Vigelandsanlegget
Hours of entertainment among 212 outdoor sculptures, a lake and sprawling parkland. (p66)

Slottsparken These stately gardens surrounding the Royal Palace are an attraction in themselves. (p34)

Botanical Garden You can be fascinated by the collection of rare trees from around the world,

or just enjoy a picnic among the flowerbeds. (p108)

Parliament Building
One of Europe's more charming parliaments is a delight to explore. (p37)

Akerselva River Once a polluted industrial waterway, today the Akerselva's rapids, falls and forested banks provide a surprisingly wild retreat. (p87)

Best
Parks

NENAD NEDOMACKI/SHUTTERSTOCK ©

Oslo is blessed with some incredibly beautiful parks which manage, in typical Norwegian style, to straddle the line between a bucolic naturalness and well-kept grace. As soon as the sun is out, this is where you'll find locals lolling, picnicking and often getting their gear off and catching some rays.

Best Art Parks

Tjuvholmen Sculpture Park If you've only got time for one art experience, this one is super stress-free and comes with beautiful Oslofjord views. (p57)

Frognerparken Yes, you're here for Gustav Vigeland's epic Vigelandsanlegget sculptures, but the park itself is also an incredibly pretty and languid spot to wander. (pictured; p70)

Ekebergparken Dark woods, lush green fields and rare geological outcrops would be enough of a draw but this hilly park is also dotted with extraordinary contemporary artworks. (p107)

Best Neighbourhood Parks

Botanical Garden An elegant, serene place with rare trees, a museum and some interesting artwork, too. (p108)

St Hanshaugen Park Relaxed and family-friendly green expanse with great views. (p116)

Akerselva River This urban river is fringed with small patches of parkland as well as the lovely grassy slopes of Grünerhagen. (p87)

Best Parkside Eats & Drinks

Ekeberg Restaurant Leafy calm and stunning views from the summer terrace here. (p109)

Handwerk The Botanical Garden's own kiosk is one of the city's most charming coffee and cake spots. (p109)

Vingen Beautiful views, smart small plates and top-notch cocktails by the sculpture park. (p60)

Gutta På Haugen Head to the deli for picnic supplies or visit their ice-cream cart before your park visit. (p121)

Best
Tours

MEL LONGHURST/VW PICS/UIG VIA GETTY IMAGES ©

Oslo has a range of guided tours that can offer greater cultural and historical insight into what is an easy-to-explore and super well organised destination, but one whose back story is not as well known as major world capitals.

Boat Trips

Boat tours along the Oslofjord include various sights along the waterfront and the museums of the Bygdøy Peninsula, as well as specialist tours for those interested in architecture. You can also DIY an island and beach itinerary using the commuter ferries that leave from Vippetangen Quay.

Crime Fiction

Fans of Norwegian crime fiction can join tours to the grim world of Jo Nesbø's detective Harry Hole. The Oslo Visitor Centre (p149) has details of various operators.

Cycling

Mountain bikers will find plenty of trails on which to keep themselves occupied in the Oslo hinterland. The tourist office has free cycling maps: *Sykkelkart Oslo* traces the bicycle lanes and paths throughout the city; and *Idrett og friluftsliv i Oslo* covers the Oslo hinterland. It also has a pamphlet called *Opplevelsesturer i Marka*, which contains six possible cycling and/or hiking itineraries within reach of Oslo. Also ask about guided rides along these paths or out into the countryside.

Best Tours

Viking Biking Guided bike tours that take you to the sights as well as pretty parks and fascinating back streets, or further afield to forests and beaches. (p37)

Oslo Promenade Friendly and fun guides will show you Oslo's city-centre sights, with lots of local lore thrown in. (p37)

Båtservice Sightseeing Offers a range of tours, from short trips to all-day voyages on a traditional schooner, as well as a fantastic hop-on, hop-off service. (p59)

Survival Guide

Survival Guide

Before You Go

When to Go

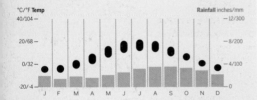

°C/°F **Temp**
40/104 —

20/68 —

0/32 —

-20/-4 —

Rainfall inches/mm
— 12/300

— 8/200

— 4/100

— 0

J F M A M J J A S O N D

Spring Flowers fill the parks in April and May, and National Day brings crowds.

Summer Days are long; Oslofjord beaches and parks are packed.

Autumn Summer's cultural calendar continues with concerts and events.

Winter The first snow falls in December; Christmas markets and concerts bring seasonal magic.

Book Your Stay

➡ Oslo has plenty of accommodation, from hostels and good chain hotels to high-end design stays.

➡ A growing number of small B&Bs and private rentals offer more character at a lower (though rarely budget) price.

➡ Hotels are usually well run and comfortable but tend towards the bland, and – yes, you guessed it – you'll pay a lot more for what you get compared with other countries.

➡ Hotel breakfasts are hearty and are increasingly included in the price, but always check.

➡ Most hotels have wi-fi access.

Useful Websites

➡ B&B Norway (www.bbnorway.com) Lists many of Norway's better-established B&Bs.

➡ Lonely Planet (lonelyplanet.com/noway/oslo/

hotels) Recommendations and bookings.

Best Budget

Ekeberg Camping (Map p18; ☎22 19 85 68; www. ekebergcamping.no; Ekebergveien 65; 2-/4-person tent 220/330kr; ⏱Jun-Aug; 🅿; 🚋Ekebergparken) Stunning natural site just minutes from the city.

Cochs Pensjonat (Map p18; ☎23 33 24 00; www.cochspensjonat.no; Parkveien 25; s/d with kitchenette from 710/940kr, without bathroom 540/750kr; 🛜; 🚋17B) Floorboards and big windows in this old-style Frogner guesthouse.

Anker Hostel (Map p18; ☎22 99 72 00; www.ankerhostel.no; Storgata 55; dm 260-300kr, s/d 620/900kr; 🛜; 🚋54) Large, well-run hostel in a perfect location between city sights and Grünerløkka going-out spots.

Best Midrange

PS: Hotell (Map p18; ☎23 15 65 00; www.pshotell. no; Maridalsveien 13c; s/d/ste 975/1390/1500kr; 🛜; 🚋54) Stylish, earthy and industrial, in a great location for eating and drinking.

Scanic Holmenkollen Park (☎22 92 20 00; www. holmenkollenparkhotel.no; Kongeveien 26; s/d 1400/1650; 🅿🛜♿; 🚋Holmen) Luxury, history and amazing views just out of the city.

Citybox Oslo (☎21 42 04 80; www.citybox.no/oslo; Prinsens gate 6; s/d 920/1045kr; 🛜; 🚋Dronningens Gate) Light, simple Scandi-style rooms in a fantastic location.

Best Top End

The Thief (Map p18; ☎24 00 40 00; www.thethief. com; Landgangen 1; d 2900-4000kr; 🛜♿; 🚋Aker brygge) Oslo's contemporary luxe choice with contemporary art cred and fabulously decorated rooms and water views.

Grand Hotel (Map p18; ☎23 21 20 00; www.grand. no; Karl Johans gate 31; d 1890-2800kr; 🅿🛜♿; 🚋Stortinget) Individually decorated, classically elegant but far from twee rooms in a historic setting.

Scandic Vulkan (☎21 05 71 00; www.scandichotels. com; Maridalsveien 13; d 1395-1700kr; 🚋54) Vintage vinyl and rustic Norwegian furniture add warmth and wit to this contemporary hotel.

Money-Saving Tips

If you're planning on a big night out, do as the locals do and *forspill* – have some pre-drink drinks at home, with either beers from the supermarket or a bottle of wine or something stronger from government-owned alcohol supermarket chain Vinmonopolet.

Arriving in Oslo

Oslo Gardermoen International Airport

Train

The fastest way into town is to catch the **Flytoget** (www.flytoget.no; adult/child 180/90kr) train, whose shuttles connect Gardermoen airport with Oslo's Central Station in just 19 minutes. Trains leave every 10 or 20 minutes between 4.40am and midnight. Some trains terminate at the Central Station, while others continue to Nationalteatret and stops to the south, terminating at Drammen.

A great money-saving tip is to hop aboard the standard **NSB** (www.nsb. no) intercity and local train services that stop at Gardermoen (93kr, from 26 minutes, hourly but fewer on Saturday). You can catch the trains at various central stations including Nationaltheatret and Oslo S. It's exactly half the price of the Fly-toget train, and nearly as fast; the trade-off is that it runs less frequently.

Bus

Flybussen (www.flybussen. no; 160kr), runs from the airport to the bus termi-nal at Galleri Oslo, as well as a few other stops in the city, every 20 minutes from 4am to around 10pm. Times vary a little depending on the day of the week; see website for a full schedule. The trip takes about 40 minutes.

Vippetangen Quay

Ferries operated by **DFDS Seaways** (www.dfds seaways.com; Vippetangen 2; 60) connect Oslo daily with Denmark from the **Vippetangen Quay** (Map p18) off Skippergata. Bus 60 stops within a couple of minutes' walk of the terminal.

Galleri Oslo Bus Terminal

All international and long-distance buses arrive and depart from the **Galleri Oslo Bus Terminal** (Map p18; 23 00 24 00; Schweigaards gate 8; Sentralstasjon). The train and bus stations are linked via a convenient overhead walkway for easy connections.

Getting Around

Tram

Oslo's tram network is extensive and runs 24 hours. Like all city public transport, it's part of the **Ruter** (https://ruter.no/ en/) ticketing system; schedules and route maps are available online or at **Trafikanten** (177; www.ruter.no; Jernbanetorget; 7am-8pm Mon-Fri, 8am-6pm Sat & Sun).

T-bane

The six-line Tunnelbanen underground system, better known as the T-bane, is faster and extends further from the city centre than most city buses or tram lines.

All T-bane lines pass

through the National-theatret, Stortinget and Jernbanetorget (for Oslo S) stations. Ruter tickets for trips in zone 1 (most of the city centre) cost adult/child 33/167kr if bought in advance (from T-bane ticket machines, 7-Elevens, Narvesen and Trafikanten).

Bicycle

Oslo City Bike (915 89 700; https://oslobysykkel.no) gives you unlimited rides of 45-minute duration over either 24 hours, three days or the season (45/99/299kr) from bicycle stands around the city. You can buy a pass via the website and your smartphone, via the app or by getting a pin from the website. The bikes are convenient and well maintained, but are only available from 6am to midnight and only in the 'ice-free' season (April to December).

Bus

There's no central, local bus station, but most buses converge at Jern-banetorget in front of Oslo S. Most westbound buses, including those to Bygdøy and Vigeland Park, also stop immediately south of the National Theatre.

Service frequency drops dramatically at night, but on weekends the night buses N12, N14 and N18 follow the tram routes until 4am or later; there are also weekend night buses (201 to 218). Oslo Pass holders can travel for free on all daytime routes in the city centre.

Boat

Ferries to the Oslofjord islands sail from Vippetangen Quay. Ferry 91 (☎23 35 68 90; on board adult/child 50/25kr, from kiosks on departure jetty adult/child 30/15kr, with Oslo Pass free) to Bygdøy (March to October only) leaves from Rådhusbrygge Quay (Map p33).

Boat 62 connects Oslo with Drøbak and other Oslofjord stops en route, including Håøya for swimming and camping. It departs from Aker Brygge Pier (Map p33).

Essential Information

Business Hours

The following standard opening hours are for

Dos & Don'ts

Give thanks A *tusen takk* (thanks very much) in shops and restaurants never goes astray, even if all else is in English.

Manners Norwegians are reserved but unfailingly polite.

Respect Norwegian men are brought up to be extremely respectful of women; in bars or other social places, women usually have to make the first move.

Self-reliance Norwegians assume that you're fine unless you directly ask for help, but once you've done so they are usually more than willing to be of assistance.

high season (mid-June to mid-September).

Banks 8.15am to 3pm Monday to Wednesday and Friday, 8.15am to 5pm Thursday

Post Offices 8am to 8pm Monday to Friday, 9am to 6pm Saturday

Restaurants noon to 3pm and 6pm to 11pm

Shops 10am to 5pm Monday to Wednesday and Friday, 10am to 7pm Thursday, 10am to 2pm Saturday

Supermarkets 9am to 9pm Monday to Friday, 9am to 6pm Saturday

Vinmonopolet 10am to 5pm Monday to

Wednesday, 10am to 6pm Thursday and Friday, 10am to 3pm Saturday

Discount Cards

The **Oslo Pass** (www.visit oslo.com/en/activities-and-attractions/oslo-pass; 1/2/3 days adult 395/595/745kr, child 210/295/370kr), sold at the tourist office, is a good way of cutting transport and ticket costs around the city. The majority of the city's museums are free with the pass, as is public transport within the city limits (barring late-night buses). Other perks include restaurant and tour discounts.

Electricity

Money

➡ Banks with ATMs can be found throughout the city centre.

➡ Most shops, restaurants, bars and cafes prefer debit or credit cards over cash, even for small purchases.

Public Holidays

New Year's Day (Nyttårsdag) 1 January

Maundy Thursday (Skjærtorsdag) March/April

Good Friday (Langfredag) March/April

Easter Monday (Annen Påskedag) March/April

Labour Day (Første Mai, Arbeidsdag) 1 May

Constitution Day (Nasjonaldag) 17 May

Ascension Day (Kristi Himmelfartsdag) May/June, 40th day after Easter

Whit Monday (Annen Pinsedag) May/June, 8th Monday after Easter

Christmas Day (Første Juledag) 25 December

Boxing Day (Annen Juledag) 26 December

Safe Travel

➡ Oslo is a very safe city with low levels of street crime.

➡ East Oslo has a poor reputation and its fair share of drug addicts and homeless people; it's generally safe but can feel threatening very late at night.

➡ If you're planning on taking to Oslo's waterways or hiking up in the hills, remember that the weather here can, even in summer, change rapidly.

➡ Drugs may be readily available, but they aren't, in fact, legal.

Toilets

There are free public toilets (often called WC) near most of the major sights.

Tourist Information

Oso Visitor Centre (Map p18; ☎ 81 53 05 55; www.visitoslo.com; Jernbanetorget 1; ⏰ 9am-6pm; ☒ Sentralstasjon) is right beside the main train station. It sells transport tickets as well as the useful Oslo Pass (p147) and publishes free guides to the city.

Travellers with Disabilities

➡ Oslo is generally well set up for travellers with disabilities, and all newly constructed public buildings are required by law to have wheelchair access.

➡ Most of the major sights in the city are at least partially accessible to wheelchairs. That said, as in most countries, the situation remains a work in progress.

➡ The Oslo Visitor Centre has a list of accessible hotels and hostels, but your best bet is to contact the **Norwegian Association for the Disabled** (Norges Handikapforbund; Map p18; ☎ 24 10 24 00; www.nhf. no; Schweigaards gate 12, Grønland; ☒ 34).

➡ The **Flytoget** (www.flyto get.no; adult/child 180/90kr) train service is fully accessible for wheelchair users. Contact a station attendant for assistance with the built-in ramp.

➡ Oslo's newer trams have low floors and are easy to access for the mobility impaired.

➡ Nearly all street crossings are equipped with either a ramp or a very low kerb, and crossing signals produce an audible signal.

Visas

Norway is a party to the Schengen Convention, along with a number of other European countries. Citizens of Iceland, EU countries and other Schengen countries do not require a visa. Citizens or residents of Australia, Canada, Israel, Japan, New Zealand and the USA do not require a visa for tourist visits of up to 90 days.

Language

The official language of Norway is Norwegian, which belongs to the North Germanic (or Scandinavian) group of languages.

There are two official written forms of Norwegian, known as *Bokmål* (literally 'book language') and *Nynorsk* (or 'new Norwegian'). They are actually quite similar and understood by all speakers. Both varieties are written standards, and are used in written communication (in schools, administration and the media), whereas the spoken language has numerous local dialects. *Bokmål* is predominant in the cities, while *Nynorsk* is more common in the western fjords and the central mountains. It's estimated that out of the five million speakers of Norwegian around 85% use *Bokmål* and about 15% use *Nynorsk*. In this chapter we've used *Bokmål* only.

To enhance your trip with a phrasebook, visit **lonelyplanet.com**. Lonely Planet iPhone phrasebooks are available through the Apple App store.

Basics

Hello
God dag   go·daag

Goodbye
Ha det   haa·de

Yes
Ja   yaa

No
Nei   ney

Thank you
Taak   tak

Please
Vær så snill   veyr saw snil

You're welcome
Ingen årsak   ing·en awr·saak

Excuse me
Unnskyld   ewn·shewl

Sorry
Beklager   bey·klaa·geyr

How are you?
Hvordan har du det?
vor·dan haar doo de

Fine, thanks. And you?
Bra, takk. Og du?
braa tak aw doo

Directions

Where is ...?
Hvor er ...?   vor ayr ...

What is the address?
Hva er adressen?   va ayr aa·dre·seyn

Could you write it down, please?
Kan du skrive det?   kan doo skree·ve de

Can you show me (on the map)?
Kan du vise meg   kan du vee·se ma
(på kartet)?   (paw kar·te)

Eating & Drinking

A table for (four), please.
Et bord til (fire), takk   et bawr til
(fee·re)   tak

What would you recommend?
Hva vil du anbefale?   va vil doo an·be·fa·le

What does it include?
Hva inkluderer det?   va in·kloo·dey·re de

I don't eat (meat).

Jeg spise ikke (kjøtt).

yai (*spi*·se) i·key (sheut)

I'd like the bill, please.

Kan jeg få regningen, takk

kan yai faw *rai*·ning·en tak

Shopping

I'm looking for ...
Jeg leter etter cyai ley·ter e·ter ...

May I look at it?
Kan jeg få se på det? kan yai faw se
paw de

How much is it?

Hvor mye koster det? vor mew·e
kaws·ter de

Emergencies

Help	*Hjelp!*	yelp
Go away!	*Forsvinn!*	fawr·svin
I'm lost.	*Jeg har gått meg vill.*	
	yai har gawl rnai vil	
Call ...!	*Ring ...!*	ring
a doctor	*en lege*	cn le·ge
the police	*politiet*	po·lee·tee·ay

Time & Numbers

What time is it?
Hva er klokka? vaa eyr *klaw*·ka

It's (two) o'clock
Klokka er (to). *klaw*·ka eyr (taw)

in the morning
awm *fawr*·mi·dan *om formiddagen.*

in the afternoon
awm e·ter·mi·dan *om ettermiddagen*

1	*en*	en
2	*to*	taw
3	*tre*	trey
4	*fire*	fee·re
5	*fem*	fem
6	*seks*	seks
7	*sju*	shoo
8	*åtte*	aw·te
9	*ni*	nee
10	*ti*	tee
100	*hundre*	hun·dre
1000	*tusen*	tu·sen

Transport & Directions

I want to go to ...
Jeg skal til ... yai skaal til ...

At what time does it arrive/leave?
Når ankommer/ nawr an·kaw·mer/
går den? gawr den

Does it stop at (Majorstua)?
Stopper denne på staw·per dey·ne paw
(Majorstua)? (maa·yoor·stu·a)

Please tell me when we get to (Oslo).
Kan du si fra når kan doo see fraa nawr
vi kommer til (Oslo)? vee kaw·mer til
(os·law)

Please stop here.
Vær så snill å stoppe her.
veyr saw snil aw *sto*·pe heyr

one-way ticket
en·*veys*·bee·let *enveisbillett*

return ticket
re·*toor*·bee·let *returbillett*

boat	*båt*	bawt
bus	*buss*	bus
plane	*fly*	flew
taxi	*drosje*	draw·shey
train	*tåg*	tawg

Behind the Scenes

Send Us Your Feedback

We love to hear from travellers – your comments help make our books better. We read every word, and we guarantee that your feedback goes straight to the authors. Visit **lonelyplanet.com/contact** to submit your updates and suggestions.

Note: We may edit, reproduce and incorporate your comments in Lonely Planet products such as guidebooks, websites and digital products, so let us know if you don't want your comments reproduced or your name acknowledged. For a copy of our privacy policy visit lonelyplanet.com/privacy.

Acknowledgements

Cover photograph: Oslo Opera House, Nanisimova/Shutterstock ©

Contents photograph: Aker Brygge, Kiev. Victor/Shutterstock ©

Donna's Thanks

I'm ever grateful to the city of Oslo, possibly the kindest, most decent place on earth. I am incredibly indebted to Arvild Bruun and to Barry Kavanagh for such inspiring leads, and for the delightful company. Thanks also to dear friend Daniel Nettheim for another weekend wander, Claudia Van Tunen for your hospitality, and to Chris Wareing, Mark Steiner and Hugo Race for the music. And as ever, thanks to Joe Guario in Melbourne for your love through the wires.

This Book

This 1st edition of Lonely Planet's *Pocket Oslo* guidebook was researched and written by Donna Wheeler. This guidebook was produced by the following:

Destination Editor Gemma Graham

Product Editors Genna Patterson, Susan Paterson

Senior Cartographers Valentina Kremenchutskaya, David Kemp

Book Designer Fergal Condon

Assisting Editor Janet Austin, Andrea Dobbin

Assisting Cartographer Wayne Murphy

Cover Researcher Naomi Parker

Thanks to Jennifer Carey, Jo Cooke, Gwen Cotter, Helen Elfer, Sandie Kestell, Claire Naylor, Karyn Noble, Anne Mason, Anthony Phelan, Doug Rimington, Angela Tinson, Sam Wheeler, Tony Wheeler

Index

See also separate subindexes for:

⊗ **Eating p155**

☺ **Drinking p156**

✪ **Entertainment p156**

🔒 **Shopping p156**

🍴 Eating

SORINA CHIRITA

LONELY PLANET IN THE WILD

Send your 'Lonely Planet in the Wild' photos to social@lonelyplanet.com
We share the best on our Facebook page every week!

Our Writers

Donna Wheeler

Donna has written guidebooks for Lonely Planet for over ten years, including the *Italy*, *Norway*, *Belgium*, *Africa*, *Tunisia*, *Algeria*, *France*, *Austria* and *Australia* titles. She became a travel writer after various careers as a commissioning editor, creative director, digital producer and content strategist. Born and bred in Sydney, Australia, Donna fell in love with Melbourne's moody bluestone streets as a teenage art student. She has divided her time between there and her beloved home town for over two decades, along with residential stints in Turin, Paris, Bordeaux, New York, London and rural Ireland. Donna travels widely (and deeply) in Europe, North Africa, the US and Asia.

Published by Lonely Planet Global Limited
CRN 554153
1st edition – April 2018
ISBN 978 1 78701 122 9
© Lonely Planet 2018   Photographs © as indicated 2018
10 9 8 7 6 5 4 3 2 1
Printed in China

Although the authors and Lonely Planet have taken all reasonable care in preparing this book, we make no warranty about the accuracy or completeness of its content and, to the maximum extent permitted, disclaim all liability arising from its use.

All rights reserved. No part of this publication may be copied, stored in a retrieval system, or transmitted in any form by any means, electronic, mechanical, recording or otherwise, except brief extracts for the purpose of review, and no part of this publication may be sold or hired, without the written permission of the publisher. Lonely Planet and the Lonely Planet logo are trademarks of Lonely Planet and are registered in the US Patent and Trademark Office and in other countries. Lonely Planet does not allow its name or logo to be appropriated by commercial establishments, such as retailers, restaurants or hotels. Please let us know of any misuses: lonelyplanet.com/ip.